HOW TO START A REAL ESTATE BUSINESS

Your Step -By- Step Guide To Building Wealth Through Investment

Jeanelle K. Douglas

Copyright © 2024 by Jeanelle K. Douglas. All rights reserved. No part of this book, HOW TO START A REAL ESTATE BUSINESS, may be reproduced, stored in a retrieval system, or transmitted in any form or by any means, electronic, mechanical, photocopying, recording, or otherwise, without the prior written permission of the author, Jeanelle K. Douglas.

Table of Contents

Introduction 6

    Unlocking Your Real Estate Dreams 6

    Understanding the Real Estate Industry 8

    Why start a real estate business? 10

Establishing the Foundation Setting the foundation 14

    Defining Your Vision and Goals 19

    Market Research and Analysis 22

    Legal and Regulatory Considerations 26

    Crafting Your Business Plan 33

    Elements of Comprehensive Real Estate Business Plan 37

    Setting financial objectives and projections 42

    Developing Your Unique Value Proposition 45

    Identify your unique strengths and differentiators 46

Financing Your Venture 51

    Budgeting and managing cash flows 56

    Starting a Real Estate Business: Understanding Debt vs. Equity Financing 60

    When Beginning a Real Estate Business 63

- Considerations and implication 65
- Building Your Team 67
  - Identifying key roles and responsibilities 71
  - Hiring employees versus independent contractors 76
  - The advantages of hiring employees 77
  - Challenges in Hiring Employees 78
  - Benefits of Independent Contractors 79
  - Challenges for Independent Contractors 81
  - Building relationships with partners and suppliers 82
- Establishing Your Brand 86
  - Developing a memorable brand identity 90
  - Creating Marketing Strategies to Launch a Real Estate Business 95
  - Using digital platforms for promotion 99
- Finding Properties 104
  - Strategies for Property Acquisition 108
  - Conducting Property Due Diligence 113
  - Negotiating Deals and Contracts for Starting a Real Estate Business 118
- Managing Property 124

Setting Up Property Management Systems 128

Managing tenant relations and leases 132

Ensures property maintenance and upkeep 135

Scaling Your Business 138

Growth and Expansion Strategies in the Real Estate Business 142

Scaling operations efficiently 148

Managing risks and challenges 153

Managing Legal and Ethical Issues 158

Ensuring compliance with real estate laws and regulations. ... 162

Ethical Conduct in Real Estate Transactions 166

Dealing With Disputes And Legal Issues. 170

Thriving in the Real Estate Industry 174

Keeping Up With Market Trends 179

Networking and developing industry relationships. 183

Continuous Education and Professional Development 187

Conclusion 191

Reflecting on your journey 192

Introduction

Unlocking Your Real Estate Dreams

Welcome to the world of real estate business, where every transaction represents a new opportunity, and each property serves as a canvas for your ideas. If you've ever wanted to get into the exciting and profitable world of real estate, this book is your vital guide to success.

In this book, we take a trip that goes beyond the typical limitations of entrepreneurship. This book guides you through every step of the exciting yet challenging process of starting and expanding your own real estate enterprise, whether you're a seasoned investor diversifying your portfolio or a beginner entering the market.

The choice to invest in real estate is more than just financial; it's a leap of faith into a world where innovation meets tradition and profit intersects with community building. With the correct techniques, mentality, and resources, you have the ability to turn your dreams into concrete assets that not only provide financial rewards but also have a long-term influence on the landscape of your local community.

In these pages, you'll learn the fundamental ideas and practical insights required to manage the many parts of the real estate market. Each chapter methodically provides you with the information and confidence you need to succeed in this competitive environment, from developing a strong business strategy to obtaining finance, from developing your brand identity to efficiently managing properties.

But beneath the practicalities of property acquisition and financial administration, there is a deeper story of passion, resilience, and the never-ending quest for perfection. As you begin on this path, keep in mind that success in real estate is about more than simply statistics; it's about making important relationships, embracing innovation, and leaving a legacy that goes well beyond the bounds of brick and paper.

So, whether you're ready to take your first steps into the world of real estate or want to take your current operations to new heights, "How to Start a Real Estate Business" is your must-have guide on this exciting journey. Let's take this revolutionary journey together and open the door to your real estate aspirations.

Understanding the Real Estate Industry

The real estate sector is a complicated and dynamic environment that includes a wide range of operations, including property development and management, sales, leasing, and investing. Real estate is primarily concerned with the purchase, sale, and leasing of properties such as residential, commercial, industrial, and unoccupied. However, it goes well beyond basic transactions; it influences the physical world we live in, fuels economic progress, and reflects society's ever-changing demands and desires.

Recognizing the real estate industry's cyclical nature is critical for understanding its complexities. Market circumstances change in response to a variety of variables, including economic indicators, demographic changes, government policies, and international events. Understanding these cycles is critical for managing the industry's ebbs and flows, whether it's capturing chances during times of growth or enduring downturns with resilience and adaptively.

Real estate inextricably links to other areas of the economy, impacting fields such as construction, finance, technology, and urban planning. This interconnection emphasizes the significance of remaining alert to wider socioeconomic trends and upcoming innovations that will define the future of real estate.

In addition to its economic significance, the real estate business has enormous cultural and social worth. Properties are more than simply physical structures; they are places where people and communities live, work, and socialize. As a result, successful real estate firms understand the value of establishing sustainable and dynamic communities, as well as developing locations that improve quality of life while also promoting inclusion, diversity, and sustainability.

Furthermore, the real estate business has a wide range of players, including developers, investors, brokers, tenants, homeowners, and municipal governments. Each participant has a distinct impact on the industry's dynamics and outcomes, emphasizing the significance of teamwork, communication, and relationship-building when navigating the intricate web of real estate transactions and operations.

Finally, technology improvements have transformed the way real estate companies function, ushering in a new era of digital disruption and creativity. From online property listings and virtual tours to block- chain-based transactions and predictive analytics, technology has altered every element of the real estate lifecycle, creating new potential for efficiency, transparency, and market insights.

To summarize, knowing the real estate sector takes more than just technical knowledge; it also necessitates a comprehensive comprehension of its economic, social, and cultural components. By embracing its complexities and dynamics, aspiring real estate entrepreneurs can position themselves to navigate the industry's challenges while capitalizing on its numerous opportunities, laying the groundwork for a successful and fulfilling career in real estate entrepreneurship.

Why start a real estate business?

There are several compelling reasons to start a real estate firm, each of which appeals to a distinct set of aspirations, goals, and personal circumstances. Let's look at some of the primary reasons for going on this business journey:

1. **Financial Independence:** Real estate has long been seen as a means to financial independence. Unlike many other businesses, real estate investments have the ability to provide passive income streams that may sustain a comfortable lifestyle while also increasing long-term wealth. Whether through rental properties, property flipping, or real estate development, the opportunity to produce consistent cash flow and amass equity is a key motivator for many ambitious entrepreneurs.

2. **Flexibility and Control:** One of the most appealing parts of beginning a real estate business is the freedom that it provides. As your own boss, you may create your own schedule, pick your tasks, and steer the course of your business. Whether you like to work alone or with a team, real estate entrepreneurship offers a degree of autonomy and control that is frequently unavailable in typical working environments.
3. **Tangible Assets and Wealth Building:** Real estate investments are based on tangible assets, which are properties that have inherent worth and may grow over time. Unlike stocks and other financial instruments, which are susceptible to market volatility, real estate gives a feeling of security and stability, as well as a practical path to growing wealth and leaving a legacy for future generations.
4. **Diversification and Portfolio Growth:** For investors looking to diversify their portfolios, real estate is an appealing alternative asset class. Individuals can reduce risk and improve overall portfolio performance by including real estate holdings in their investment mix, especially during periods of economic instability. Real estate investments may also provide tax advantages and

inflation-hedging benefits, adding to their appeal as a strategic component of a diversified investment plan.

5. **Opportunities for Creativity and Innovation:** Real estate entrepreneurship is a dynamic and creative business in which individuals may demonstrate their vision, creativity, and innovation. Real estate businesses may leave a lasting impression on the physical environment by constructing distinctive living spaces, regenerating abandoned communities, or applying sustainable building methods.

6. **Community influence and empowerment:** Aside from financial concerns, real estate entrepreneurship has the potential to have a significant influence on communities. Real estate entrepreneurs may help their areas' social and economic vitality by restoring derelict sites, offering affordable housing alternatives, or developing attractive mixed-use complexes, instilling a sense of community pride and empowerment.

7. **Lifelong Learning and Personal Growth:** Starting a real estate firm is more than simply attaining financial success; it is also a path of personal development and self-awareness. From understanding the complexities of property management and negotiation to polishing interpersonal and leadership skills, real estate

entrepreneurship is a never-ending learning curve that requires individuals to adapt and improve their talents.

Various financial goals, lifestyle preferences, and personal beliefs influence the decision to establish a real estate firm. Whether pursuing financial independence, artistic fulfillment, or community impact, real estate entrepreneurship provides a wide range of options for individuals to explore their passions, achieve their goals, and leave a lasting legacy in the ever-changing real estate market.

Establishing the Foundation

Setting the foundation

Creating the basis for your real estate firm is similar to building the framework for a strong and durable edifice. To ensure a strong start and long-term success, you must define your vision, explain your goals, perform extensive market research, and handle legal and regulatory constraints.

It is critical to clearly explain your goal for the real estate industry from the start. What is your venture's overarching goal and mission?

Are you interested in offering affordable housing options, reviving urban districts, or building luxury properties?

Clarifying your vision not only drives business decisions, but it also acts as a light of inspiration and motivation for stakeholders ranging from investors to workers and community members.

With your vision in place, the next stage is to establish specific and attainable goals for your real estate firm. Whether it's purchasing a particular number of properties within a set timeframe, earning a target annual income, or expanding into new areas, objectives give a road map for advancement and allow you to track your progress along the way. Furthermore, breaking down bigger goals into smaller, achievable actions will help you stay focused and motivated while transforming dreams into concrete results.

Market research is an essential component of laying the groundwork for your real estate firm. It entails researching local market trends, identifying possible opportunities and problems, determining client wants and preferences, and assessing the competitive environment. Conducting extensive market research provides significant insights that help you make crucial company decisions, including property acquisition plans, pricing techniques, and marketing approaches. Furthermore, remaining informed about macroeconomic trends, demographic shifts, and regulatory changes enables you to forecast market dynamics and adjust your company plans accordingly.

Navigating the legal and regulatory landscape is another critical component of laying the groundwork for your real estate firm. The real estate business is subject to several legal and regulatory restrictions, ranging from zoning rules and construction codes to landlord-tenant legislation and property tax policies. Ensuring compliance with applicable rules and regulations not only protects your company from potential liabilities and fines but also fosters confidence and credibility among stakeholders such as investors, consumers, and regulatory agencies. Consulting with legal professionals and seeking professional advice can help you navigate the complexities of the legal landscape and establish a strong legal foundation for your real estate firm.

Let's go further into laying the groundwork for your real estate business.

Aside from defining your vision, creating goals, performing market research, and resolving legal concerns, there are numerous more factors to consider while laying the framework for your venture:

1. Financial preparation: Creating a profitable real estate business necessitates meticulous financial preparation. This includes evaluating initial expenses, finding prospective funding sources, developing a budget, and forecasting cash flow. Understanding your financial needs and restrictions is critical for making sound decisions regarding property purchase, development, and operating costs.

2. Identifying Target Markets: When performing market research, it is critical to identify and analyze your target markets. This includes knowing your target audience's demographics, interests, and demands, whether they are first-time homeowners, business renters, or investors. Tailoring your services and marketing methods to your target market's individual demands will help you compete and succeed.

3. Networking and Building Relationships: Real estate is a relationship-driven profession, and networking is essential for growing your business. Establishing connections with industry specialists, such as real estate agents, brokers, contractors, and bankers, may lead to beneficial cooperation, recommendations, and insights. Attending industry events, joining professional groups, and using online networking platforms may all help you build your network and make significant contacts.

4. Technology and Systems: Adopting technology and building effective systems is critical for simplifying operations and increasing efficiency in your real estate organization. From property management software and customer relationship management (CRM) systems to digital marketing tools and virtual reality (VR) technologies for property tours, technology may help you increase productivity, improve the client experience, and remain ahead of the competition.

5. Risk Management: Real estate investing carries inherent risks, such as market swings and property vacancies, as well as regulatory changes and unanticipated costs. Creating a risk management strategy that identifies possible risks, analyzes their effects, and describes mitigation actions is critical to protecting your organization and assets. This might include diversifying your assets, having proper insurance coverage, and keeping financial reserves for emergencies.

6. Continuous Learning and Adaptation: Technological improvements, market trends, and regulatory changes all contribute to the ongoing evolution of the real estate sector. As a real estate entrepreneur, you must cultivate a mindset of continual learning and adaptability. Keeping up with industry changes, attending seminars and workshops, and seeking mentoring from experienced experts will help you stay ahead of the competition and adjust your plans to changing market conditions.

Laying the groundwork for your real estate business extends beyond the early phases of defining your vision and goals, performing market research, and resolving legal concerns. It entails meticulous financial planning, identifying target markets, networking, adopting technology, controlling risks, and cultivating a culture of continual learning and adaptability. By creating a solid foundation, you may position your real estate company for long-term success and resilience in the dynamic and competitive real estate market.

Defining Your Vision and Goals

Every decision and activity in any successful real estate firm is guided by a clear and appealing vision paired with well-defined goals. Defining your vision is analogous to painting a clear image of the future you aim to build, while creating goals gives you the blueprint for making that vision a reality.

1. **Crafting Your Vision:**

    Your vision is the overarching purpose and mission that propel your real estate firm forward. It encompasses the essential beliefs, ideals, and objectives that define what your organization stands for and the effect it aspires to create. Crafting a compelling vision entails thinking about your personal beliefs, ambitions, and objectives, as well as analyzing the needs and desires of your target market and community. Your vision should excite and drive stakeholders, from workers and investors to consumers and partners, uniting them behind a shared purpose and direction. Whether it's regenerating urban districts, delivering affordable housing alternatives, or establishing sustainable and inclusive communities, your vision acts as the North Star that leads your real estate journey.

2. Setting SMART objectives:

Once you have a clear vision in place, the next step is to transform that vision into practical objectives that are specific, measurable, achievable, relevant, and time-bound (SMART). SMART goals give a framework for defining clear targets, measuring progress, and holding oneself accountable for achievements. When defining goals for your real estate firm, consider aspects such as property acquisition targets, revenue estimates, market share ambitions, customer satisfaction measurements, and community impact goals. Breaking down your goal into precise, realistic milestones builds a roadmap for development and ensures that your efforts are connected with your ultimate vision and purpose.

3. Aligning Vision and Goals:

It's crucial to maintain alignment between your vision and goals to develop coherence and harmony in your real estate firm. Ensure your goals directly align with and support your broader vision, highlighting the key values and ideas that drive your organization. Regularly examining and refining your vision and goals helps you respond to changing market conditions, developing trends, and growing stakeholder demands, ensuring that your real estate firm stays relevant and sensitive to the industry's dynamic environment.

4. Communicating Your Vision and Objectives:

Effective communication is crucial to rallying stakeholders around your vision and objectives and promoting alignment and participation within your real estate firm. Articulating your vision and goals clearly and compellingly to workers, investors, customers, and partners fosters a shared sense of purpose and direction, encouraging dedication and collaboration. Utilize numerous communication channels, such as meetings, presentations, newsletters, and social media, to continually reaffirm your vision and goals and keep stakeholders informed and engaged.

In conclusion, identifying your vision and goals is a vital stage in launching a real estate firm. Your vision offers a broad purpose and direction for your firm, while SMART goals transform that vision into achievable objectives. By aligning your objectives with your vision, communicating effectively, and continuously revisiting and refining your vision and goals, you build a roadmap for success and lay the groundwork for a profitable and meaningful real estate enterprise.

Market Research and Analysis

In the field of real estate entrepreneurship, market research and analysis serve as the cornerstones for informed decision-making, strategic planning, and sustainable growth. Conducting extensive market research requires diving deep into the dynamics of local, regional, and national real estate markets to gather useful insights on supply and demand dynamics, price patterns, demographic shifts, and competitive landscapes. Let's look at the full process of market research and analysis and its relevance in establishing the foundation for a successful real estate firm.

1. **Understanding local market dynamics:** Real estate markets are essentially local, with distinct traits, trends, and causes that differ from one region to another. Conducting local market research entails studying aspects such as population demographics, job trends, income levels, housing preferences, and lifestyle patterns. Understanding the demand for different sorts of properties, from single-family houses to multifamily apartments, commercial spaces, and mixed-use developments, helps real estate entrepreneurs adjust their offers to match the individual requirements and preferences of local people and companies.

2. **Assessing Supply and Demand:**

A major part of market research is measuring the balance between supply and demand in the local real estate market. This entails assessing indicators like inventory levels, vacancy rates, absorption rates, and new building activity across different property types and submarkets. By evaluating the equilibrium between supply and demand, real estate entrepreneurs can discover prospective possibilities for investment, development, or property acquisition, as well as potential risks and obstacles associated with excess or undersupply in certain market sectors.

3. **Analyzing pricing trends:**

Pricing trends play a key role in evaluating the viability and profitability of real estate investments. Market research entails reviewing historical sales data, similar property transactions, and price patterns to determine the current market value of properties in your target market. This analysis helps real estate entrepreneurs make informed decisions about property acquisition, pricing strategies, and investment opportunities, ensuring that they maximize returns while mitigating risks.

4. Identifying target customer segments:

Market research enables real estate entrepreneurs to identify and target specific customer segments with tailored offerings and marketing strategies. By analyzing demographic data, lifestyle preferences, purchasing behavior, and psychographic characteristics of target customers, real estate entrepreneurs can develop a deep understanding of their needs and preferences. This allows for the creation of customized real estate solutions that resonate with target customers, whether they're first-time homebuyers, empty nesters, millennials, or businesses seeking commercial space.

5. Assessing Competitive Landscapes:

Understanding the competitive landscape is essential for effectively positioning your real estate business and differentiating your offerings in the market. Market research involves analyzing competing properties, assessing their features, amenities, pricing, and market positioning. By identifying strengths, weaknesses, opportunities, and threats posed by competitors, real estate entrepreneurs can develop unique value propositions, marketing strategies, and branding initiatives that set their business apart and attract target customers.

6. **Forecasting market trends:**

Market research also involves forecasting future market trends and anticipating shifts in demand, pricing, and market dynamics. This involves analyzing macroeconomic indicators, interest rates, employment trends, population growth projections, and regulatory changes that may impact the real estate market. By staying ahead of emerging trends and disruptions, real estate entrepreneurs can adapt their strategies proactively, capitalize on opportunities, and mitigate the risks associated with market fluctuations.

In conclusion, market research and analysis are indispensable components of starting a real estate business. By delving deep into local market dynamics, assessing supply and demand, analyzing pricing trends, identifying target customer segments, assessing competitive landscapes, and forecasting market trends, real estate entrepreneurs can make informed decisions, identify lucrative opportunities, and position their business for long-term success in the dynamic and competitive real estate industry.

Legal and Regulatory Considerations

Navigating the legal and regulatory landscape is paramount when starting a real estate business, as the industry is subject to a myriad of laws, regulations, and compliance requirements at the local, state, and federal levels. Understanding and adhering to these legal considerations is essential for ensuring compliance, protecting your business interests, and mitigating potential risks and liabilities.

1. **Entity Formation and Business Structure:** One of the first legal considerations when starting a real estate business is selecting the appropriate entity formation and business structure. This decision impacts various aspects of your business, including liability protection, tax implications, and operational flexibility. Common business structures for real estate businesses include sole proprietorships, partnerships, limited liability companies (LLCs), and corporations. Each structure has its advantages and disadvantages in terms of liability protection, taxation, and management flexibility, so it's essential to consult with legal and financial advisors to determine the best option for your specific needs and objectives.

2. **Licensing and Qualifications:**

   Depending on the nature of your real estate activities, you may need to obtain specific licenses, permits, or certifications to legally operate your business. For example, real estate agents and brokers are typically required to obtain a state-issued real estate license, while property managers may need a property management license in some jurisdictions. Additionally, certain real estate transactions, such as those involving affordable housing or commercial properties, may require specialized qualifications or certifications. It's crucial to research the licensing requirements in your state or locality and ensure that you meet all necessary qualifications before conducting any real estate transactions.

3. **Contractual Agreements and Documentation:**

   Real estate transactions involve a multitude of contractual agreements and legal documentation that govern the rights, obligations, and responsibilities of all parties involved. Whether its purchase agreements, lease agreements, property management contracts, or construction contracts, it's essential to draft clear, comprehensive, and legally enforceable agreements that protect your interests and minimize potential disputes. Working with experienced real estate attorneys or legal professionals can help ensure that your contracts and documentation comply with applicable laws and regulations and adequately safeguard your business interests.

4. **Land use and zoning regulations:**

   Land use and zoning regulations control property development, use, and modifications within specific geographic areas. These regulations dictate factors such as property setbacks, building heights, land density, and permitted land uses, among others. Understanding and complying with land use and zoning regulations is essential when acquiring, developing, or modifying real estate properties to ensure that your projects are legally permissible and compliant with local zoning ordinances and planning regulations. Consulting with land use attorneys or zoning experts can help you navigate the complexities of land use and zoning regulations and secure the necessary permits or variances for your projects.

5. **Environmental Regulations and Due Diligence:**
   Environmental regulations play a significant role in real estate transactions, particularly when acquiring or developing properties with potential environmental

liabilities or contamination issues. Conducting thorough environmental due diligence is essential to identify and assess any environmental risks associated with a property, such as soil contamination, groundwater pollution, or hazardous materials. Compliance with environmental regulations, such as the Comprehensive Environmental Response, Compensation, and Liability Act (CERCLA) and the Resource Conservation and Recovery Act (RCRA), is crucial to avoid potential legal liabilities and financial penalties. Engaging environmental consultants or specialists can help assess environmental risks and ensure compliance with applicable regulations during real estate transactions.

6. **Fair Housing and Anti-Discrimination Laws:**

   Fair housing and anti-discrimination laws prohibit discrimination based on protected characteristics such as race, color, religion, national origin, sex, familial status, and disability in housing-related activities. Real estate businesses, including landlords, property managers, and real estate agents, must comply with these laws to ensure equal housing opportunities for all individuals. Familiarizing yourself with fair housing laws, such as the Fair Housing Act (FHA) and state and local fair housing ordinances, and implementing policies and practices that promote fair and equitable treatment of tenants and homebuyers is essential to avoiding potential discrimination lawsuits or regulatory enforcement actions.

7. Taxation and Financial Compliance:
Real estate businesses are subject to various tax obligations and financial regulations at the local, state, and federal levels. Understanding the tax implications related to property ownership, rental income, capital gains, and depreciation is essential for tax planning and compliance. Additionally, real estate businesses must adhere to financial reporting requirements and maintain accurate accounting records to comply with regulatory standards and investor expectations.

8. Risk management and liability protection:
Real estate entrepreneurship involves inherent risks, including property damage, personal injury claims, tenant disputes, and legal liabilities. Implementing risk management strategies, such as obtaining adequate insurance coverage, incorporating liability protection measures, and conducting thorough due diligence on

potential risks, helps mitigate exposure to legal and financial liabilities and safeguard your business interests.

9. **Intellectual Property Protection:**
Intellectual property rights, such as trademarks, copyrights, and trade secrets, play a crucial role in protecting the branding, marketing materials, and proprietary information associated with your real estate business. Taking steps to register and protect your intellectual property assets helps prevent unauthorized use or infringement by competitors and enhances the value and marketability of your brand.

10. **Compliance with real estate laws and regulations:**
In addition to the specific legal considerations mentioned earlier, real estate businesses must comply with a wide range of laws and regulations governing real estate transactions, property management, landlord-tenant relationships, and brokerage activities. Staying abreast of changes in real estate laws and regulations, such as disclosure requirements, tenant rights, and real estate brokerage laws, is essential for maintaining legal compliance and mitigating regulatory risks.

11. Dispute Resolution and Legal Support:

Despite careful planning and adherence to legal requirements, real estate businesses may encounter disputes, disagreements, or legal challenges during their operations. Having access to legal support and resources, such as experienced real estate attorneys or dispute resolution professionals, is essential for resolving conflicts effectively, protecting your legal rights, and minimizing potential legal exposure or financial losses.

Addressing these additional legal and regulatory considerations, real estate entrepreneurs can enhance their understanding of the legal landscape and implement proactive measures to ensure compliance, protect their business interests, and mitigate risks effectively, thereby laying a robust legal foundation for their ventures.

Crafting Your Business Plan

Starting a real estate firm requires creating a detailed business plan that details your vision, goals, tactics, and financial predictions. A well-crafted business plan is a guiding document that explains your company's concept, market opportunity, competitive advantage, and growth strategy to potential investors, partners, and stakeholders. Let's look at the important elements of developing a strong business plan for your real estate firm.

1. **Executive Summary:**

    The executive summary provides a brief overview of your real estate business plan, emphasizing essential elements such as your business concept, market opportunity, competitive advantage, target market, and financial predictions. This part offers visitors an overview of your company and lays the groundwork for the comprehensive information that follows.

2. **Business description and vision:**

    In this area, describe your real estate business vision, as well as your company's idea, goal, and values in depth. Describe the real estate operations you want to pursue, such as property development, property management, real estate brokerage, or a mix of services. To separate your firm from the competition, clearly identify your target market, geographic focus, and unique areas of competence.

3. Market Analysis:

Perform a detailed market study to determine the current situation of the real estate market and identify potential opportunities and difficulties. Analyze local market trends, demand-supply dynamics, demographic patterns, and competitive landscapes to better understand market viability and positioning. In your target market, identify target client categories, market niches, and undiscovered growth potential.

4. Competitive analysis:

Conduct a complete competitive study to determine your rivals' strengths, weaknesses, opportunities, and threats. Identify and evaluate significant rivals in your target market, including their market positioning, offers, pricing strategies, and consumer interaction approaches. Identify gaps or opportunities for your real estate firm to differentiate itself and obtain a competitive advantage.

5. Marketing and Sales Strategies:

Outline your marketing and sales plan for attracting and retaining consumers, generating leads, and increasing revenue. Define your branding, messaging, and positioning strategies to help your real estate firm stand out in the market. Outline your marketing channels, such as digital marketing, social media, networking events, and referrals, as well as your sales methods, which may include direct sales, partnerships, and customer relationship management.

6. Operations and management:

Describe the operational structure and management team of your real estate company, including important persons, positions, and duties. Describe your organizational structure, decision-making processes, and methods for overseeing day-to-day operations, property purchases, leasing activities, and tenant interactions. Highlight any strategic partnerships, alliances, or outsourcing agreements that help you achieve operational efficiency and scalability.

7. Financial projections:

Create thorough financial predictions that estimate your real estate business's financial success and sustainability. Include income statements, cash flow estimates, balance sheets, and essential financial metrics like ROI, NPV, and IRR. Consider property purchase costs, development costs, operational expenditures, rental income, and sales or leasing revenue sources.

8. Risk management and contingency planning:
Identify possible risks and uncertainties that may affect your real estate business, and create contingency plans to successfully reduce them. Consider market volatility, regulatory changes, economic downturns, property vacancies, tenant defaults, and unexpected costs. Develop risk-mitigation techniques such as diversification, insurance coverage, financial reserves, and alternate exit routes.

Finally, creating a business plan for your real estate endeavor requires extensive research, strategic planning, and financial forecasting in order to successfully communicate your vision, goals, and tactics. A well-written business plan acts as a road map for success, guiding your real estate company through its genesis, development, and expansion phases while positioning it for long-term sustainability and profitability in the dynamic and competitive real estate sector.

Elements of Comprehensive Real Estate Business Plan

Creating a detailed business plan for your real estate enterprise is a critical step toward success in today's dynamic and competitive real estate sector. This document is a plan that details your vision, tactics, and financial predictions, offering a road map for accomplishing your business goals. Let's go over the main components of a real estate business plan in detail:

Executive Summary: The executive summary captures the core of your real estate business plan by providing a succinct review of your company's concept, market potential, competitive advantage, and financial predictions. It offers readers an overview of your vision and goals, laying the groundwork for the comprehensive information that follows.

Business Description: This part should contain a full explanation of your real estate business concept, including its goal, vision, and fundamental values. Define the real estate operations you want to pursue, such as property development, property management, real estate brokerage, or a mix of these. To separate your company from the competition, define your target market, geographic focus, and particular areas of specialty.

Market Analysis: Perform a detailed market study to determine the current situation of the real estate market and identify potential opportunities and difficulties. Analyze local market trends, demand-supply dynamics, demographic patterns, and competitive landscapes to better understand market viability and positioning. In your target market, identify target client categories, market niches, and undiscovered growth potential.

Competitive analysis: Conduct a complete competitive study to determine your rivals' strengths, weaknesses, opportunities, and threats. Identify and evaluate significant rivals in your target market, including their market positioning, offers, pricing strategies, and consumer interaction approaches. Identify gaps or opportunities for your real estate firm to differentiate itself and obtain a competitive advantage.

Marketing and Sales Strategies: Outline your marketing and sales plan for attracting and retaining consumers, generating leads, and increasing revenue. Define your branding, messaging, and positioning strategies to help your real estate firm stand out in the market. Determine your target client categories and establish your marketing methods, including digital marketing, social media, networking events, and referrals. Describe your sales strategies, including direct sales, partnerships, and customer relationship management.

Operations and management: Describe the operational structure and management team of your real estate company, including important persons, positions, and duties. Describe your organizational structure, decision-making processes, and methods for overseeing day-to-day operations, property purchases, leasing activities, and tenant interactions. Highlight any strategic partnerships, alliances, or outsourcing agreements that help you achieve operational efficiency and scalability.

Financial projections: Create thorough financial predictions that estimate your real estate business's financial success and sustainability. Include income statements, cash flow estimates, balance sheets, and essential financial metrics like ROI, NPV, and IRR. Consider property purchase costs, development costs, operational expenditures, rental income, and sales or leasing revenue sources.

Risk management and contingency planning: Identify possible risks and uncertainties that may affect your real estate business, and create contingency plans to successfully reduce them. Consider market volatility, regulatory changes, economic downturns, property vacancies, tenant defaults, and unexpected costs. Develop risk-mitigation techniques such as diversification, insurance coverage, financial reserves, and alternate exit routes.

Other issues to consider exist beyond the fundamental components covered in the provided material regarding a real estate business plan.

Legal and Regulatory Compliance: Ensure that your business strategy includes real estate-specific legal and regulatory needs, such as licenses, permits, zoning restrictions, fair housing legislation, and environmental standards. Compliance with these standards is critical to functioning lawfully and avoiding potential legal problems.

Technology and Innovation: Discuss how you will incorporate technology and innovation into your real estate operations to increase efficiency, improve the customer experience, and remain competitive. Consider incorporating technology into your company strategy, such as property management software, virtual reality for property tours, and internet marketing tools.

Sustainability and Environmental Responsibility: Explain how your real estate company will integrate sustainability concepts and environmental stewardship into its operations and property development initiatives. Consider techniques like energy-efficient building design, green building certification, and sustainable property management.

Community Engagement and Social Responsibility: Describe your real estate company's dedication to community involvement and social responsibility. Discuss efforts like affordable housing developments, community development programs, and collaborations with local groups to address social and economic concerns in the places where you work.

Exit Strategy: Include an exit strategy in your business plan that details potential exit situations as well as methods for selling assets or exiting the firm. When establishing your exit strategy, take into account market circumstances, investment deadlines, and personal or financial goals.

Addressing these additional components in your real estate business plan helps you create a more comprehensive and robust roadmap for your enterprise, ensuring that all major concerns are considered throughout the strategic planning process.

Setting financial objectives and projections

When launching a real estate firm, it is critical to establish clear financial goals and predictions in order to design a course for success and ensure the venture's long-term survival. This includes setting realistic financial targets, forecasting income streams and costs, and creating a strategic strategy to attain your financial goals. Let's go over the process of establishing financial objectives and predictions in detail:

1. **Setting Financial Goals:** Begin by determining your financial objectives for the real estate business. Consider both short-term and long-term goals, such as revenue, profitability, ROI, and growth indicators. Your financial objectives should be consistent with your entire business vision and purpose, representing the results and milestones you hope to reach as you create and expand your real estate firm.

2. **Identifying Revenue Streams:** Next, determine your real estate business's major revenue streams. This could include property sales, rental income from investment properties, property management fees, brokerage commissions, development profits, or any other revenue streams relevant to your company model. Consider how

each revenue source might help you achieve your overall financial objectives and predictions.

3. Projection of Income and Expenses:

Create accurate financial estimates for your real estate firm, including both income and costs. Use possible revenue from property sales, rental income, brokerage commissions, and other sources. Similarly, project expenses include property acquisition, development, operation, and marketing costs, as well as staffing and administrative charges. Be cautious in your forecasts and include contingencies to cover unexpected costs or revenue variations.

4. Cash-flow Management:

Cash flow management is critical to the financial health and longevity of any real estate firm. Plan and manage your cash flow to ensure that you have enough money to fulfill operational expenditures, debt service payments, and investment demands. Implement effective cash flow management procedures, such as budgeting, cost tracking, receivables management, and proactive debt management, to maintain a good cash flow position and reduce financial risk.

5. Risk Assessment and Mitigation:

Determine any risks and uncertainties that may affect your financial objectives and estimates. Assess the risks associated with market volatility, economic downturns, regulatory changes, tenant defaults, property vacancies, and other real estate-specific issues. Develop solutions to limit these risks, such as diversification, insurance coverage, contingency planning, and proactive risk management procedures, to ensure your financial stability and company interests.

6. Monitoring and Adjustment:

Monitor your financial performance on a regular basis in relation to your goals and expectations, and make any modifications. Examine your financial accounts, cash flow predictions, and key performance indicators to gauge progress and find opportunities for improvement. To stay on track to meet your financial objectives, be prepared to change your strategy, update your predictions, and make course corrections in response to changing market circumstances, emerging opportunities, or unexpected problems.

Setting financial objectives and making predictions is an important part of launching a real estate firm. Establishing clear financial objectives, identifying revenue streams, projecting income and expenses, effectively managing cash flow, assessing and mitigating risks, and monitoring performance can all help you lay the groundwork for financial success and sustainability in the dynamic and competitive real estate industry.

Developing Your Unique Value Proposition

In the competitive real estate sector, having a distinct value proposition is critical for differentiating your company and attracting clients, investors, and partners. Your unique value proposition is the promise of value you provide to your target market, separating your real estate firm from rivals while also addressing your clients' individual wants and preferences. Here's how to create a compelling and unique value proposition for your real estate business:

To effectively serve your target market with real estate services, first get a thorough grasp of the people, firms, or demographics you seek to serve. Conduct market research to determine their requirements, preferences, pain points, and goals in relation to real estate transactions. Understanding your target market's motives and issues allows you to design your value offering to meet their individual demands and provide answers to their worries.

Identify your unique strengths and differentiators

Consider your real estate company's distinct qualities, competencies, and assets that set it apart from rivals. This might include specialized experience in a certain market sector or property type, a track record of successful transactions, access to rare properties or investment possibilities, cutting-edge technology or tools, great customer service, or a distinct corporate identity. Determine what distinguishes your real estate business, and use these qualities to differentiate yourself in the market.

Consider your target market's unmet demands, issues, and pain points related to the real estate sector. Your value proposition should include solutions or perks that satisfy your clients' unique demands and ease their pain points. Whether it's providing personalized guidance and support throughout the buying or selling process, offering flexible financing options, or leveraging technology to streamline transactions and improve convenience, figure out how your real estate company can add value and solve problems for your clients.

Communicate clear benefits and outcomes: Use your value proposition to clearly express the benefits and outcomes that your real estate firm provides to clients, investors, and partners. Focus on the actual results, value, and effect that clients may expect from working with you, whether it's achieving their real estate investment goals, optimizing property transaction profits, reducing risk, or improving their entire real estate experience. Explain how your unique capabilities and solutions translate into tangible advantages and outcomes for your target audience.

To stand out, create a powerful brand identity and message that reflect your unique value proposition and appeal to your target market. Your branding should reflect your real estate company's personality, values, and market positioning, while your messaging should clearly and effectively express your value offer. Use appealing language, imagery, and narrative to elicit emotion and connect with your audience on a deeper level, emphasizing the unique benefits and value you provide.

Developing a distinctive value offer demands continuing evolution and adaptability to changing market dynamics, client needs, and the competitive environment. Stay up-to-date on industry trends, client and stakeholder input, and new opportunities to refine and improve your value proposition over time. By constantly inventing and adapting, you can keep your real estate firm current, competitive, and appealing in an ever-changing real estate market.

Finally, creating a compelling and distinct value offer is critical for success in the real estate sector. Understanding your target market, identifying your unique strengths and differentiators, addressing unmet needs or pain points, communicating clear benefits and outcomes, differentiating through branding and messaging, and constantly evolving and adapting will enable you to create a compelling value proposition that distinguishes your real estate business and resonates with your target market, positioning you for success in the competitive real estate landscape.

The material provided covers major parts of establishing a distinct value proposition for a real estate firm, but other factors are worth exploring:

Client Testimonial and Success Stories: Include client testimonials and success stories in your messages. Real-life examples of delighted clients who have benefited from your unique value proposition may help your brand gain credibility and authenticity, supporting the concrete outcomes and good experiences it offers.

Emphasize trust and honesty in your value proposition: Emphasize open and ethical business methods, a commitment to client pleasure, and a desire to develop long-term partnerships built on trust. Trust is an important aspect in real estate deals, and stressing it may be a significant distinction.

Educational resources and expertise: Establish your real estate firm as a reliable source of industry knowledge and experience. Provide educational tools, insights, and market knowledge to your customers, demonstrating your dedication to keeping them informed and empowered throughout the real estate transaction.

New Technology and Products: Explain how your real estate firm stands out with new technology or products. This might include advanced analytics, virtual reality property tours, user-friendly applications, and other technological solutions that improve the customer experience and speed real estate transactions.

Community Engagement and Social Responsibility: If your real estate company actively participates in community participation or social responsibility programs, include this in your value proposition. Highlighting your dedication to giving back or helping with community development might appeal to clients who respect socially responsible enterprises.

Personalized service and client-centered approach: Promote a customized approach to client service. Highlight how your real estate firm customizes its services to match each client's specific needs and preferences. Communicate your client-centric emphasis, whether it is through tailored property suggestions, marketing initiatives, or investment advice.

Keep in mind that you can refine a successful value proposition as a dynamic component of your business strategy based on market input, changing industry trends, and shifting customer expectations. Regularly analyze the success of your value proposition and be willing to make changes to ensure that it remains current and attractive in an ever-changing real estate environment.

Financing Your Venture

Starting a real estate firm necessitates a considerable capital commitment to cover different components of the endeavor, such as property acquisitions, development projects, operational expenditures, marketing initiatives, and employee salaries. Securing sufficient financing is critical for starting and growing your real estate firm, and entrepreneurs in the real estate market have a variety of financing options. Let's look at these funding possibilities in detail:

Equity Financing: Equity financing is the process of obtaining funds by selling ownership stakes in your real estate company to investors in exchange for equity shares. Private equity investors, venture capitalists, angel investors, or collaborations with real estate investment businesses can achieve this. Equity financing provides funding without the obligation to repay, but it also entails sharing ownership and even giving up some control over your organization.

Debt Financing: Borrowing funds from lenders or financial institutions with the responsibility to return the principle amount plus interest over a predetermined period. Commercial loans, mortgage loans, lines of credit, and real estate crowdfunding platforms are popular types of debt financing for real estate firms.

Debt financing allows you to keep complete ownership and management of your company but also necessitates frequent loan repayments, which might impact cash flow and financial flexibility.

Self-financing: Self-financing is the use of personal money, assets, or resources to support a real estate endeavor. This may entail using personal savings, retirement money, home equity, or other personal assets to cover starting costs and initial investments. Self-financing gives you complete control and ownership of your firm without having to rely on external investors or lenders, but it also carries personal financial risk and may limit the amount of funds available for investment.

Joint Ventures and Partnerships: Joint ventures and partnerships entail partnering with other real estate investors, developers, and enterprises to pool resources, exchange knowledge, and co-fund real estate projects or initiatives. Joint venture partners may provide finance, land, or skills in exchange for a portion of the earnings or an ownership stake in the enterprise. Partnerships can help you gain access to more finance, resources, and market possibilities while distributing risks and using complementary strengths.

Government Programs and Incentives: Grants, subsidies, tax credits, and low-interest loans can promote real estate development, affordable housing, and regeneration activities in certain locations. Investigate federal, state, and municipal government programs that provide financial aid or incentives to real estate enterprises, including eligibility requirements and application processes.

Real Estate Investment Trusts (REITs): These publicly listed firms own, operate, or finance income-generating assets. Individuals can participate in real estate investment trusts (REITs) without personally owning or managing properties. Consider investing in REITs as a passive way to diversify your real estate portfolio and produce income while avoiding the operational obligations of owning actual assets.

Crowd-funding and Peer-to-Peer Lending: Real estate businesses can raise financing from a huge number of individual investors or lenders using internet platforms. These platforms connect real estate projects or initiatives with potential investors or lenders who provide funding in exchange for equity interests, debt instruments, or return on investment. Crowdfunding and peer-to-peer lending provide alternatives to established financial institutions.

Sponsorship and Financing: Sponsorship is the act of working with sponsors, such as businesses, brands, or individuals, to provide financial support or sponsorship in exchange for branding opportunities, advertising exposure, or other promotional benefits related to your real estate projects or initiatives. Sponsorship finance allows you to use external sponsors to support your real estate activities in exchange for marketing awareness and brand exposure.

Funding your real estate endeavor necessitates a careful examination of numerous financing choices and techniques in order to get the required funds for starting and developing your firm. Whether you choose stock financing, debt financing, self-financing, joint ventures, government programs, REITs, crowdsourcing, sponsorship, or a combination of these alternatives, the best financing strategy relies on your company's goals, financial needs, risk tolerance, and development plans. By researching and utilizing various financing sources and structures, you can efficiently fund your real estate endeavor and position it for success in the competitive real estate market.

Exploring Financing Options: When launching a real estate firm, it is critical to research and understand the numerous funding choices accessible to ensure the venture's success and sustainability. Real estate businesses need considerable financial commitment, and obtaining appropriate finance is critical for paying property acquisitions, development projects, operations expenses, marketing initiatives, and employee salaries.

Budgeting and managing cash flows

Starting and operating a successful real estate firm requires careful budgeting and cash flow management. Effective budgeting ensures efficient allocation of resources, while cash flow management guarantees sufficient liquidity for funding costs and investments.

Budgeting: Budgeting is the process of devising a comprehensive strategy for allocating financial resources across various parts of your real estate firm. It enables you to prioritize spending, create financial goals, and track costs to ensure that you live within your means and make sound financial decisions.

Here are some significant budgetary considerations:

Start with a Comprehensive Company Plan: Your company plan serves as the foundation for your budgeting efforts. It covers your company's objectives, target market, revenue predictions, and costs. Use this strategy to identify major areas for funding, such as property acquisitions, marketing, staffing, and operating costs.

Estimate Startup Costs: Determine the initial expenses necessary to start your real estate firm, such as license fees, permits, equipment, office space, marketing materials, and professional services. To create a realistic budget, take into account both one-time and continuous running expenses.

Forecast Revenue Streams: Determine the prospective revenue streams for your real estate firm, such as property sales, rental income, management fees, brokerage commissions, and development profits. Using market research and historical data, establish reasonable revenue predictions based on market demand and industry trends.

Identify fixed and variable expenditures: In your budget, separate fixed expenditures (e.g., rent, salary, utilities) from variable expenses (e.g., marketing, maintenance, repairs). This helps you prioritize necessary costs while still having the freedom to change discretionary spending as required.

Allocate finances intelligently depending on your company's priorities and ambitions. Concentrate on investments that will add long-term value and help your real estate company's development and sustainability. Prioritize expenditures based on considerations such as possible ROI, market demand, and competitive advantage. Managing cash flow: Managing cash flow entails tracking the input and outflow of cash in your real estate firm to ensure that you have enough liquidity to satisfy financial commitments and capitalize on investment possibilities.

Here are some essential ways to manage cash flow effectively:

1. Create a cash flow projection that estimates your expected cash inflows and outflows over a set time period, such as monthly or quarterly. Include income predictions, operational expenditures, loan payments, taxes, and other financial commitments to account for future cash shortages or surpluses.

2. Accounts receivable and payable should be closely monitored. Implement effective invoicing and payment collection systems to reduce delays in collecting payments from customers or tenants, as well as negotiate acceptable payment terms with suppliers and vendors.

3. Control Operating Expenses: Optimize operational efficiency, negotiate contracts and agreements with vendors, and implement cost-cutting measures wherever possible. On a regular basis, review and assess your spending to identify areas for cost savings or optimization without sacrificing quality or service standards.

4. Maintain Cash Reserves: Set aside enough cash to meet unexpected costs, emergencies, or periods of poor cash flow. Create a cash reserve fund or line of credit to provide a financial cushion and ensure that you can meet your financial obligations even in difficult times.

5. Monitor and change: Regularly compare your cash flow performance to your forecasts, and change your budget and expenditures as appropriate. Identify trends, patterns, or anomalies in your cash flow data, and take proactive steps to resolve issues or capitalize on opportunities to improve cash flow management.

Implementing efficient budgeting and cash flow management methods will help you secure your real estate company's financial health and stability, navigate problems, and capitalize on possibilities for development and success in the competitive real estate sector.

Starting a Real Estate Business: Understanding Debt vs. Equity Financing

Debt and equity finance are two key techniques that real estate entrepreneurs might employ to support their operations. Each option has its advantages, concerns, and ramifications, and understanding the distinctions between debt and equity financing is vital for making informed financial decisions when beginning a real estate firm.

Let's delve deeper into the complexities of debt and equity financing when starting a real estate business:

Debt Financing: Debt financing is the process of borrowing money from lenders or financial institutions and repaying the principle plus interest over a certain period of time. Real estate businesses can acquire debt financing through different sources, including commercial banks, mortgage lenders, and private lenders, and real estate crowd-funding sites.

Here are crucial features of debt financing when beginning a real estate business:

Repayment Obligation: Debt financing compels the borrower to repay the borrowed capital, often in regular payments over a predetermined period. This payback obligation includes both the principal amount borrowed and interest payments, which are dependent on the agreed-upon interest rate and loan terms.

Lenders may require collateral: such as the real estate property being financed or other assets possessed by the borrower, to secure the debt. Collateral acts as security for the loan and gives lenders recourse in the event of failure, allowing them to seize and sell the collateral to reclaim their investment.

Fixed or Variable Interest Rates: Debt finance offers both fixed-rate and variable-rate loan choices. Fixed-rate loans maintain a stable interest rate throughout the loan period, offering predictability and consistency in monthly payments. Variable-rate loans, on the other hand, have an interest rate that swings depending on market circumstances, giving borrowers the opportunity for lower starting rates but exposing them to interest rate risk.

Leverage: Debt financing allows real estate entrepreneurs to leverage their investments by borrowing cash to finance a portion of the property acquisition price. By leveraging leverage, businesses may multiply their returns on investment and boost their purchasing power, thus creating bigger profits from real estate deals.

Risk of Default: One of the key hazards associated with debt financing is the risk of default, in which the borrower fails to return the loan according to the agreed-upon conditions. Default can result in serious repercussions, including foreclosure, loss of collateral, harm to credit scores, and legal action by lenders to recover outstanding obligations.

Equity Financing: Equity financing entails obtaining funds by selling ownership holdings in a real estate firm to investors in exchange for equity shares. Real estate entrepreneurs can receive equity funding through many sources, including private equity investors, venture capitalists, angel investors, real estate investment trusts (REITs), and partnerships with real estate investment firms. Here are crucial components of equity financing.

When Beginning a Real Estate Business

Ownership Stake: Equity financing entails selling the real estate firm's ownership interests or shares to investors in exchange for funding. Investors become shareholders in the firm and partake in the earnings, losses, and risks involved with the enterprise. Equity investors may also have voting rights and influence over corporate decisions, depending on the conditions of the investment agreement.

No Repayment Obligation: Unlike debt financing, equity financing does not compel the borrower to repay the invested capital. Equity investors provide capital without the expectation of return, bearing the risk of future losses in exchange for the opportunity to participate in the business's success and share in the profits earned.

Dilution of Ownership: Equity financing involves diluting the ownership interests of the real estate enterprise's original founders or owners. Entrepreneurs sacrifice a portion of their ownership and influence over the firm by selling equity shares to investors, potentially compromising decision-making authority and managerial duties.

Opportunity for Better Returns: Equity financing offers the opportunity for better returns on investment compared to debt financing. Since equity investors participate in the firm's profits and development, they stand to benefit from the rise in the value of real estate assets and the success of the business over time.

Long-Term Commitment: Equity financing often includes a long-term commitment from investors, since they become shareholders in the firm and expect to collect returns on their investment over a prolonged period of time. Real estate entrepreneurs must assess the effects of equity financing on their business's ownership structure, governance, and strategic direction.

Considerations and implication

When picking between debt and equity funding for starting a real estate firm, entrepreneurs need to carefully evaluate the following factors:

Financial goals and ambitions: Assess your financial goals, risk tolerance, and long-term ambitions for the real estate firm. Determine if you prefer preserving ownership and control (equity financing) or leveraging borrowed cash (debt financing) to reach your financial goals.

Capital Structure: Evaluate the appropriate capital structure for your real estate firm, considering the balance between debt and equity funding. Striking the appropriate balance guarantees that you have sufficient cash to support investments while controlling financial risk and preserving flexibility in your business operations.

Cost of Capital: Compare the expenses associated with debt and equity financing, including interest rates, loan terms, equity dilution, and investor expectations. When assessing your financing options, consider the impact of financing expenses on your total profitability and return on investment.

Risk Management: Assess the risks associated with debt and equity financing, including default risk, interest rate risk, liquidity risk, and equity dilution risk. Develop risk management techniques to limit potential hazards and maintain your real estate firm's financial health and stability.

Investor Relations: Consider the effects of equity funding on investor relations, communication, and governance. Establish clear and effective communication channels with equity investors, addressing their expectations, offering frequent updates on company performance, and creating trust and confidence in your real estate enterprise.

Understanding the distinctions between debt and equity financing is vital for real estate entrepreneurs when launching a real estate firm. Both strategies provide various advantages and concerns, and entrepreneurs must carefully analyze their funding needs, financial goals, risk tolerance, and long-term ambitions to identify the most acceptable financing plan for their firm. By assessing the consequences of debt and equity financing and making informed financial decisions, entrepreneurs may establish the framework for a successful and sustainable real estate firm.

Building Your Team

Launching and sustaining a successful real estate firm necessitates collecting a qualified and dependable team of experts who can offer their experience, abilities, and knowledge to all elements of the operation. Building the appropriate team is critical for reaching corporate goals, providing outstanding service to customers, and navigating the complexity of the real estate market. Here's a thorough look at assembling your team while beginning a real estate business:

1. **Identify key roles and responsibilities:**

    Begin by determining the core roles and tasks needed to run your real estate firm successfully. These may include real estate agents, property managers, administrative workers, marketing specialists, financial consultants, legal advisors, and property maintenance and remodeling contractors or tradesmen.

2. **Recruitment and Hiring Procedures:**

    Create a disciplined recruiting and hiring process to attract and choose the best candidates for your company. This procedure may include advertising job positions through multiple sources, holding interviews, evaluating individuals' credentials and abilities, and performing background or reference checks as necessary. Look for individuals who not only have the requisite talents and experience but also share your company's values and culture.

3. **Networking and Referral:**

   Use your professional network and industry contacts to find suitable team members. Attend real estate networking events, conferences, and industry meetings to meet professionals and connect with possible collaborators, partners, and employees. Seek recommendations from trustworthy colleagues, mentors, and industry peers who can suggest suitable recruits for your team.

4. **Training and Development:**

   Invest in continuing training and development programs to provide your team members with the information, skills, and tools they require to succeed in their jobs. Provide training on real estate rules and regulations, sales methods, customer service, property management best practices, marketing strategies, and any other areas that are pertinent to their professional development and success.

5. **Encourage collaboration and communication:**

   Create a culture of cooperation, open communication, and teamwork among your real estate professionals. Encourage regular team meetings, brainstorming sessions, and idea-sharing forums to foster cooperation and innovation.

Establish open lines of communication and welcome comments, recommendations, and constructive criticism in order to consistently enhance team relations and productivity.

6. **Promote Customer Service Excellence:**

   Prioritize customer service quality and client satisfaction as essential principles for your real estate firm. Ensure that team members understand the significance of providing outstanding service to clients and prioritize developing strong relationships based on trust, honesty, and integrity. Encourage your employees to go above and beyond to meet customer demands and exceed expectations at all times.

7. **Delegate tasks and empower team members:**

   Delegate duties and responsibilities properly so that team members may take responsibility for their jobs and contribute to the company's success. Provide clear leadership, direction, and support while simultaneously encouraging autonomy and initiative to instill a feeling of ownership and accountability in team members. Recognize and recognize team members for their efforts and accomplishments to inspire and incentivize performance.

8. Promote a Positive Work Environment:

Create a pleasant work atmosphere that promotes diversity, inclusion, and mutual respect among team members. Create an environment of support, recognition, and appreciation in which team members feel valued, driven, and empowered to achieve. Encourage work-life balance, employee well-being, and professional development opportunities to increase job satisfaction and retention among your real estate team members.

By carefully choosing, supporting, and empowering your team members, you can create a strong, cohesive, and high-performing team that drives your real estate company's success and development. Invest in hiring top personnel, offering continuing training and support, cultivating a great work culture, and encouraging cooperation and communication to create a team that is devoted, motivated, and capable of meeting your business objectives in the competitive real estate sector.

Identifying key roles and responsibilities

When launching a real estate firm, it is critical to determine important roles and duties in order to successfully structure your team and cover all parts of the business. Each function is crucial to the company's performance, and identifying defined tasks helps to streamline processes, enhance efficiency, and create accountability among team members. Let's look at some of the most prevalent positions and tasks in the real estate business:

1. **Real Estate Agent:**

   Responsibilities: Assist customers in purchasing, selling, or renting residential or commercial properties.
   - Assist customers with property appraisal, market analysis, and pricing strategy.
   - Arrange property showings, negotiate, and arrange deals.
   - Provide information about real estate rules, regulations, and commercial agreements.
   - Establish and develop connections with clients, prospects, and industry professionals.

2. **Property Manager:**
   - Responsibilities: Manage rental properties on behalf of owners.
   - Manage tenant relationships, lease agreements, and rent collection.
   - Coordinate property upkeep, repairs, and inspections.
   - Manage the vacancy, advertising, and tenant screening procedures.
   - Ensure that local legislation and best practices for property management are followed.

3. **Administration Staff:**
   - Responsibilities include administrative assistance for real estate agents and management staff.
   - Oversee office operations, such as arranging appointments, answering phones, and processing letters.
   - Manage client databases, files, and records.
   - Assist with marketing initiatives, such as creating promotional materials and arranging advertising campaigns.
   - Manage standard office activities such as filing, data entry, and office supply inventory.

4. **Marketing Specialist:**

Responsibilities include creating and implementing a marketing strategy to showcase properties and attract clients.

- Create engaging property listings, brochures, and marketing materials.
- Manage your online presence, which includes website content, social media, and digital advertising.
- Arrange photography, videography, and virtual tours of properties.
- Analyze market trends, track competitor activity, and find marketing possibilities.

5. **Finance Advisor:**

Responsibilities: Offer financial counsel and advice to customers on real estate investments.

- Help customers with budgeting, financial planning, and mortgage finance choices.
- Evaluate investment possibilities, analyze risks, and suggest investment methods.
- Stay informed on tax rules, investment regulations, and financial market developments.
- Work with real estate agents and clients to maximize financial results.

6. **Legal Counsel: Responsibilities:**
    - Offer legal advice and representation for real estate transactions and contracts.
    - Review and create purchase agreements, leasing agreements, and other legal papers.
    - Perform due diligence on properties, such as title searches and property surveys.
    - Handle real estate-related issues, discussions, and resolutions.
    - Ensure adherence to real estate rules, regulations, and ethical standards.

7. **Contractors/Traders:**
    - Responsibilities include doing construction, remodeling, and upkeep on properties.
    - Manage repairs, upgrades, and enhancements to increase property value.
    - Work with property managers and real estate agents to resolve maintenance concerns.
    - Provide estimates, timetables, and high-quality craftsmanship for property improvements.
    - Ensure adherence to construction rules, safety laws, and industry standards.

8. **Support staff (e.g., receptionist, office manager):**
    - Responsibilities include administrative assistance for the real estate team and management.
    - Greet clients, answer phones, and handle office correspondence.
    - Set up appointments, meetings, and property showings.
    - Assist with office organizing, filing, and data entry. Manage office logistics, such as supply, equipment, and facility management.
    - Identifying these important duties and responsibilities is crucial for establishing your real estate team and ensuring that all aspects of your business are properly addressed. By establishing clear roles and duties, you can streamline processes, increase productivity, and build a collaborative and efficient work atmosphere in your real estate firm.

Hiring employees versus independent contractors

Hiring employees vs. independent contractors to start a real estate business.

As you commence on the adventure of creating a real estate firm, one of the most important decisions you'll make is whether to recruit employees or work with independent contractors to grow your team. This decision can have a substantial impact on your company's structure, operations, expenses, and legal duties.

Let's get into the fascinating issue of recruiting workers vs. independent contractors in the context of beginning a real estate firm.

Hiring Employees: Build a team of motivated specialists to help you reach your real estate goals on a daily basis. This is the appeal of employing staff. When you recruit personnel, you have the potential to establish a coherent team culture, encourage cooperation, and focus everyone's efforts on a shared goal. Employees become committed to the success of your company, bringing their talents, knowledge, and passion to the table.

The advantages of hiring employees

1. **Loyalty and Commitment:** Employees that have been with your company for a long time are more likely to display loyalty and commitment. They are more likely to align with your company's beliefs, goals, and objectives, devoting their talents and efforts to achieve common success.
2. **Control and Management:** Hiring people gives you more control over their job activities, timetables, and performance. You may provide direct supervision, training, and feedback to ensure that employees achieve your goals.
3. **Team Collaboration:** Employees promote camaraderie and teamwork within your real estate company by working on projects, exchanging ideas, and supporting one another's efforts. A cohesive team atmosphere fosters creativity, productivity, and a favorable workplace culture.
4. **Brand Representation:** Your employees serve as brand ambassadors for your real estate company, promoting your brand and values to customers, prospects, and industry professionals. Their professionalism, knowledge, and

devotion enhance your company's reputation and brand image.

Challenges in Hiring Employees

1. **Higher Costs:** Hiring workers incurs extra costs beyond their compensation, such as payroll taxes, perks (such as health insurance and retirement contributions), paid time off, and other employee-related expenses. These charges might have a substantial influence on your budget and cash flow.
2. **Legal Obligations:** As an employer, you must comply with labor laws, employment rules, and workplace standards regarding hiring, compensation, benefits, working conditions, and termination. Failure to comply with legal responsibilities may result in penalties, fines, or legal challenges.
3. **Administrative Burden:** Managing personnel entails administrative activities such as payroll processing, tax withholding, benefit administration, and compliance reporting. This administrative load can be time-consuming

and complex, necessitating meticulous attention to detail and strict adherence to regulatory guidelines.

Consider hiring independent contractors to help your real estate firm. Independent contractors provide flexibility, specialized experience, and a cost-effective alternative for certain projects or activities without requiring a long-term commitment from employees. They work as self-employed professionals, offering services on a contract basis while maintaining freedom and autonomy.

Benefits of Independent Contractors

- Flexibility and Scalability: Independent contractors allow you to scale your staff up or down based on project requirements and business expectations. You can hire contractors for specific projects, short-term assignments, or on an as-needed basis without being bound by long-term employment obligations.
- Particular Expertise: Independent contractors bring particular skills, knowledge, and

experience to the table, allowing you to tap into expertise that may not be accessible in-house. Contractors provide specialized talents and industry knowledge that supplement your team's strengths and improve project results.

- Cost savings: recruiting independent contractors can be less expensive than recruiting full-time workers since it eliminates continuing payroll taxes, benefits, and other employee-related costs. Contractors are self-employed and must pay their own taxes, insurance, and overhead expenses.
- Reduced Administrative Load: Working with independent contractors minimizes your administrative load because you do not have to manage payroll, benefits, tax withholding, or other employee-related chores. Contractors manage their own company operations, allowing you to concentrate on essential business tasks.

Challenges for Independent Contractors

1. Limited Control: Independent contractors work as independent professionals, with complete control over their work techniques, timelines, and deliverables. While this provides flexibility, it may result in workers having less direct control over project execution and quality.
2. Compliance Risks: Misclassification of independent contractors may lead to legal and compliance issues for your real estate organization. Contractors must classify themselves properly using legal criteria such as control over work, independence, and commercial relationships to avoid potential penalties or legal issues.
3. Availability and Reliability: Independent contractors may have other customers and responsibilities, which could cause availability and scheduling difficulties. Clear definition of project timeframes, deliverables, and expectations ensures reliable and timely completion of work.

When deciding whether to hire employees or independent contractors for your real estate firm, evaluate your needs, project requirements, budget, and long-term goals. To decide the appropriate technique for team formation, consider the nature of the task, the amount of control required, the skill needs, and the resources available. Finally, when launching a real estate firm, the decision between recruiting staff and working with independent contractors is critical and must be carefully considered and strategically planned. Your business objectives, tastes, and circumstances determine the best option among the distinct advantages and disadvantages of both solutions. By analyzing the advantages and disadvantages of each technique and connecting your team-building strategy with your company goals, you can lay the groundwork for success and development in the competitive real estate sector.

Building relationships with partners and suppliers

Imagine starting your real estate firm as a strategic collaborator, supported by a network of trustworthy partners and suppliers. Cultivating great relationships with partners and suppliers is about more than simply transactions; it's about creating long-term partnerships based on trust, mutual respect, and shared goals. Building connections in the real estate industry can lay the groundwork for success, unlocking new opportunities, enhancing skills, and fostering growth. Let's look at the fascinating process of building connections with partners and suppliers while launching a real estate business:

1. Strategic Partnerships: Cultivating strategic connections with other firms, organizations, or individuals in the real estate ecosystem may open up a world of possibilities for your business. Strategic partnerships, such as collaborating with local developers, builders, architects, or interior designers; forming alliances with mortgage brokers, lenders, or financial institutions; or establishing affiliations with real estate associations or professional networks, can help you expand your reach, improve your services, and stand out in the market.

2. Win-Win Collaborations: When building connections with partners, aim to create win-win collaborations that benefit all parties involved. Identify synergies and complementary qualities where collaboration can benefit both your firm and your partners. Whether it's through collaborative marketing initiatives, co-hosting events, pooling resources, or cross-referring clients, look for ways to benefit from each other's knowledge and networks.

3. Open communication and transparency: Building great relationships with partners and suppliers demands open communication, openness, and honesty. Create a trusting and collaborative workplace by maintaining open lines of communication, sharing pertinent information, and proactively resolving any issues or problems. Establish clear expectations, openly communicate goals and objectives, and maintain transparency in your interactions to foster trust and improve your connections over time.

4. Delivering Value: Building successful connections with partners and suppliers requires showcasing your value proposition and dedication to providing excellent value. Whether it's giving timely updates, providing important insights and market knowledge, or delivering high-quality products and services, prioritizing surpassing expectations and constantly delivering value can help you enhance your reputation and trust with your partners.

5. Building rapport: Relationship development with partners and suppliers is about more than simply commercial transactions; it's about developing true rapport and connections with people. Take the time to get to know your partners on a personal level, grasp

their objectives, difficulties, and aspirations, and demonstrate real concern for their success. Building rapport and cultivating positive relationships based on mutual respect and camaraderie can pave the way for successful collaborations and long-term partnerships.

6. Promoting Long-Term Relationships: Instead of focusing on short-term advantages, prioritize long-term relationships with your partners and suppliers. Invest in creating strong, long-lasting connections based on trust, dependability, and mutual support. Celebrate successes, recognize milestones, and thank your partners for their contributions to your business journey. By cultivating long-term connections, you establish the groundwork for continued development, cooperation, and shared success in the real estate market.

7. Adaptively and Flexibility: Real estate is a dynamic and ever-changing industry, so developing relationships with partners and suppliers necessitates adaptability and flexibility. Be open to changing market conditions, emerging trends, and your partners' evolving needs. Demonstrate flexibility in your approach, a willingness to innovate, and the ability to adjust your strategies to meet the changing demands of the market and your partners.

ESTABLISHING YOUR BRAND

Consider your real estate business more than just a name on a sign or a listing on a website. Consider it a powerful brand that connects with your target audience, builds trust and credibility, and distinguishes you in a crowded market. Establishing your brand is more than simply designing logos and slogans; it's about creating a compelling identity that communicates your beliefs, skills, and unique offering to potential clients and partners. Let's embark on an exciting journey to develop your brand while starting a real estate firm.

1. Define Your Brand Identity: Establishing your brand begins with defining your brand identity, which is the essence of who you are as a real estate organization. Begin by determining your essential beliefs, mission, and vision. What differentiates you from your competitors? What do you intend for your brand to represent? Define your unique selling proposition (USP), or the value you provide that no one else does. Whether it's your customized approach to client care, your experience in a certain sector, or your

dedication to innovation, your brand identity should represent what makes you unique and memorable.

2. Develop Your Brand Story: Every successful brand has a compelling story behind it—a narrative that captures the core of who you are, why you do what you do, and how you make a difference in the lives of your customers. Create a brand narrative with authenticity, passion, and purpose. Share the path that led you to start your real estate firm, the obstacles you overcame, and the values that motivate you. Your brand's story should speak to your target audience, elicit emotion, and inspire trust and connection.

3. Design Your Visual Identity: Your logo, color palette, typography, and images are vital for brand identification and distinctiveness. Invest in expert graphic design to build a visually appealing and consistent brand identity that reflects your brand personality and speaks to your target audience. Choose colors, typefaces, and imagery that are consistent with your brand's values and elicit the right emotions in your audience.

4. Create consistent brand messaging: Consistency is essential for developing a strong brand presence. Create clear and consistent brand messaging that expresses your business's promise, values, and essential themes via all

communication platforms. From your website language and social media postings to your marketing materials and client communications, make sure your message matches your brand identity and speaks to your target demographic. Consistent messaging increases brand identification, strengthens brand identity, and encourages trust and credibility among your target audience.

5. Increase your online presence: In today's digital world, your internet presence is an important part of building your brand in the real estate market. Create a professional website that highlights your brand's identity, services, listings, and customer testimonials. Use social media networks like Instagram, Facebook, LinkedIn, and Twitter to connect with your audience, publish important material, and expand your brand's reach. Use digital marketing methods like search engine optimization (SEO), content marketing, and email marketing to generate leads and build relationships with potential customers.

6. Provide an exceptional client experience: Your brand is defined not just by what you say but also by how you make people feel. Deliver excellent client experiences that reflect your brand's values and surpass client expectations at every touchpoint. Prioritize customized service, attention to detail, and response from the initial point of contact until

closing the sale to develop long-term connections with your clients. Positive client experiences not only strengthen your brand's reputation, but they also drive word-of-mouth referrals and repeat business, accelerating your real estate firm's growth.

7. Interact with your community: Establishing your brand is more than just transactions; it is also about making real ties with your community. Participate in local events, sponsorships, and community activities to demonstrate your dedication to your community and put your brand principles into action. Engage with local groups, charities, and issues that match with your brand's goal to make a positive difference and develop goodwill in your neighborhood.

8. Measure and evolve: Building a great brand is a continual process that requires regular monitoring, measurement, and modification. Monitor key performance indicators (KPIs) such as brand awareness, engagement metrics, customer happiness, and market share to assess the efficacy of your branding initiatives. Engage clients, partners, and stakeholders to gain insights into how they perceive your brand and identify areas for growth. Be willing to adapt your brand strategy, message, and tactics in response to market feedback and changing business

demands to ensure that your brand stays relevant and meaningful in the ever-changing real estate marketplace. Establishing your brand is a captivating journey that includes defining your identity, crafting your story, designing your visual identity, creating consistent messaging, expanding your online presence, providing exceptional client experiences, engaging with your community, and constantly evolving to stay ahead in the competitive real estate industry. Investing in a powerful and memorable brand that speaks to your target audience can help you differentiate your real estate firm, gain trust and credibility, and eventually achieve long-term success and development.

Developing a memorable brand identity

Consider your real estate company more than simply a name or a logo. Consider it a living, breathing organism with a distinct personality, values, and essence. Creating a memorable brand identity means creating a unique and authentic image of your company that connects with your target audience, grabs their attention, and leaves a lasting impression. It's all about influencing views, establishing trust, and standing out in a crowded marketplace. Let's begin the exciting process of building a unique brand identity for your real estate business.

- **Define Your Brand Essence:** Begin by identifying your brand's essence, which includes the essential features, beliefs, and personality traits that distinguish your real estate firm. Consider what distinguishes your company, what values you uphold, and what feelings you want your target audience to experience. Does your company receive recognition for its dependability, professionalism, innovation, or individual service? Clarifying your brand essence creates the groundwork for developing a brand identity that connects with your target audience on a deeper level.

- Develop Your Brand Story: Every distinctive brand has a compelling story—a narrative that connects with its target audience, elicits emotion, and fosters relationships. Craft your brand's story with honesty, integrity, and purpose. Share the path that led you to start your real estate firm, the obstacles you overcame, and the values that motivate you. Your brand narrative should express your enthusiasm for real estate, your dedication to helping customers, and the distinct value you provide to the market.

- Create your visual identity: Your visual identity is a visual representation of your brand, which includes your logo, color palette, typography, and images. Invest in expert graphic design to build a visually appealing and unified brand identity that embodies your business essence and speaks to your target audience. Choose colors, typefaces, and pictures that express the required feelings and are consistent with your brand identity. Your visual identity should be consistent throughout all brand touchpoints, including your website, social media, marketing materials, and signage.
- Design a memorable logo: Your logo is the foundation of your brand identity—the visual sign that quickly conveys your business to the world. Create a distinctive logo that reflects the spirit of your real estate company and creates a lasting impact on your target audience. Whether it's a strong and modern wordmark, an exquisite insignia, or a stylized icon, your logo should be distinct, recognized, and indicative of your brand's personality. Consider collaborating with a professional designer to build a logo that speaks to

your target audience and reflects your brand's values.

- Developing Your Brand Voice: Your brand voice refers to the tone, style, and language you employ while communicating with your target audience. Create a unique brand voice that represents your brand's personality, beliefs, and target audience. Are you formal and professional, or informal and approachable? Do you employ humor, empathy, or authority in your communications? Define your brand voice and use it consistently across all communication platforms, including website writing, social media postings, client interactions, and marketing materials.

- Align Your Brand Experience: Creating a distinctive brand identity entails more than just visual aspects; it's about providing a consistent brand experience across all touchpoints. Align your brand experience with your brand essence, story, and visual identity to give your real estate firm a united and consistent image. Ensure that every engagement with your brand, whether online, in person, or via marketing communications, represents your company's values, personality, and promise to your target audience.

- Engage your audience: A memorable brand identity is one that connects with your target audience on an emotional level. Connect with your audience by using great stories, appealing images, and meaningful interactions. Use social media, content marketing, and community involvement to connect with people, form relationships, and generate brand champions. To improve your brand relationship, encourage feedback, listen to your audience, and respond sincerely to their wants and preferences.

- Evolve and adapt: Creating a distinctive brand identity is a continuous process of change and adaptation. As your real estate company develops and expands, you should continue to polish and evolve your brand identity in order to remain relevant and influential in a changing market. Monitor market trends, listen to consumer feedback, and be willing to change your brand strategy and message to fit your audience's changing requirements and preferences.

Creating Marketing Strategies to Launch a Real Estate Business

When starting a real estate firm, developing successful marketing tactics is critical to standing out in a competitive market, attracting new customers, and driving business development. These tactics provide a plan for contacting your target demographic, demonstrating your unique value offer, and eventually converting leads into loyal customers. Let's take a look at the intriguing path to building marketing tactics for starting a real estate business:

1. **Market research and analysis:** Before beginning marketing initiatives, it is critical to undertake extensive market research and analysis. This entails researching the local real estate industry, comprehending current trends, examining rival techniques, and determining your target demographic. By learning about market dynamics, consumer preferences, and competition positioning, you can customize your marketing tactics to efficiently reach and engage your target audience.

2. **Define Your Unique Selling Proposition (USP):** What distinguishes your real estate business from competitors? Define your unique selling proposition (USP), or the value proposition that distinguishes you from competitors in the market. Whether it's your customized approach to client care, specific experience in a niche industry, breakthrough technological solutions, or unique selling factors, your USP serves as the cornerstone for your marketing strategy and helps you carve out a distinct brand in the marketplace.

3. **Identify the target audience:** To develop focused marketing tactics, you must first determine your ideal target audience, which includes the demographic, psychographic, and behavioral characteristics of individuals or groups who are most likely to use your real estate services. Are you looking for first-time homebuyers, luxury property investors, commercial clientele, or a certain geographical area? Understanding your target audience allows you to adjust your messaging, platforms, and techniques to suit their requirements and preferences.

4. **Craft compelling brand messaging:** Your brand message serves as the voice of your real estate company, communicating your brand's values, personality, and value proposition to your target audience. Create a captivating brand message that connects with your target audience,

communicates your unique selling point, and motivates action. Whether you're using website content, social media postings, email campaigns, or advertising materials, your messaging should be clear, succinct, and convincing, emphasizing the advantages of working with your real estate company.

5. **Utilize multi-channel marketing:** In today's digital age, using a combination of online and offline marketing channels is critical for reaching a wide audience and increasing brand awareness. Use multi-channel marketing methods to interact with potential customers through several touchpoints. This might involve a mix of digital channels like social media marketing, content marketing, email marketing, search engine optimization (SEO), pay-per-click (PPC) advertising, and conventional channels like direct mail, print advertising, networking events, and community outreach.

6. **Content Marketing and Thought Leadership:** Content marketing is critical to establishing your real estate company as a trusted expert and thought leader in the industry. Create relevant, insightful, and entertaining content that speaks to your target audience's needs, interests, and pain areas. Whether it's blog posts, instructive guides, films, podcasts, or infographics, offer unique

insights, ideas, and resources that highlight your expertise and position your real estate company as a go-to source for helpful information.

7. **Create Relationships Through Networking:** Networking is an effective marketing technique for developing contacts, broadening your professional network, and generating real estate referrals. Attend industry events, join professional organizations, become involved in local community activities, and network with other real estate professionals, potential clients, and industry stakeholders. By developing meaningful relationships and establishing yourself as a trusted resource in your network, you may create leads, referrals, and new possibilities for your real estate company.

8. **Track, Measure, and Optimize:** Effective marketing strategies are data-driven and outcome-oriented. Implement monitoring systems and analytics tools to analyze the effectiveness of your marketing activities, track key performance indicators (KPIs), and calculate the ROI of your campaigns. Analyze indicators like website traffic, lead generation, conversion rates, customer engagement, and sales to find areas for improvement and optimize your marketing strategy for greater success.

Using digital platforms for promotion

In today's digital age, using digital platforms for promotion is critical to the success of any business, including real estate projects. These platforms provide several options to reach a larger audience, communicate with new clients, promote properties, and develop a brand presence online. Let's take a look at the fascinating world of using digital media for advertising while launching a real estate business:

1. **Site Development:** Your real estate company's website functions as a virtual shop for your brand. Many potential clients' first point of contact is your website, so invest in a professionally designed and user-friendly one. Your website should not only display your listings but also communicate your brand identity, value proposition, and unique selling qualities. Include high-quality photos, virtual tours, and extensive property descriptions to entice visitors and promote participation. To improve the user experience, make sure your website is mobile-responsive, SEO-optimized, and easy to navigate.

2. **Search Engine Optimization (SEO):** Search engine optimization (SEO) is an effective digital marketing method for enhancing your real estate company's exposure and attracting organic traffic to its website. Conduct keyword research to identify relevant search terms used by potential clients looking for real estate services in your target market. To increase your search engine rankings, include these keywords in your website's content, meta tags, and URL. Create educational and helpful material, including blog entries, neighborhood guides, and market reports, to attract visitors and build your authority in the real estate market.

3. **Social media marketing:** Social media platforms provide a dynamic and engaging environment for connecting with prospective clients, showcasing properties, and developing connections. Create professional profiles on key social networking networks, including Facebook, Instagram, Twitter, LinkedIn, and Pinterest. Share visually engaging material such as property images, videos, virtual tours, client testimonials, and real estate-related blogs. Engage your audience by swiftly replying to comments, messages, and requests. Use social media advertising alternatives, such as targeted advertisements and sponsored posts, to

reach a larger audience and generate leads for your real estate firm.

4. **Email Marketing:** Email marketing is a powerful digital marketing method for building relationships with new clients, remaining top of mind, and advertising your real estate services. Create an email list of interested prospects and previous clients through website opt-ins, open homes, and networking events. Send out frequent newsletters, property updates, market insights, and special offers to your email subscribers. Personalize your email content depending on the recipient's interests and habits to boost engagement and conversions. Track email open rates, click-through rates, and conversions to assess the efficacy of your email marketing initiatives.

5. **Online advertising:** Online advertising provides targeted and quantifiable ways to promote your real estate firm and listings to a specific audience. Consider investing in internet advertising options such as Google advertisements, social media advertisements, and display advertising to reach out to potential clients who are actively looking for real estate services or properties in your target market. Use targeting options such as geography, demographics, hobbies, and behavior to narrow down your audience and improve the success of your online advertising efforts. To

improve the effectiveness of your ad campaigns, monitor performance data such as click-through rates, conversion rates, and return on investment (ROI) to improve the effectiveness of your ad campaigns.

6. **Virtual Tour and 3D Visualization:** In the digital era, virtual tours and 3D visualization technologies have become indispensable for exhibiting properties and providing immersive experiences to prospective buyers. Invest in virtual tour software or hire experienced photographers and videographers to provide high-quality virtual tours of your properties. These virtual tours enable potential customers to explore properties from the comfort of their own homes, delivering a realistic and interactive viewing experience. Use 3D visualization tools to produce precise floor plans, renderings, and interactive property presentations that will fascinate potential buyers and differentiate your listings from the competition.

7. **Online Review and Testimonials:** Online reviews and testimonials are critical in establishing trust and credibility for your real estate firm in the digital realm. Encourage pleased customers to submit good feedback and testimonials on your website, social media pages, and third-party review sites like Google My Business, Yelp, and Zillow. Respond quickly to reviews, whether favorable or

negative, to show your dedication to customer satisfaction and resolve any problems or criticism. Display good reviews and testimonials prominently on your website and in your marketing materials to strengthen your brand's reputation and attract new customers.

In today's digital world, using digital platforms for promotion is critical for efficiently promoting your real estate firm and properties to a larger audience. You can develop a comprehensive digital marketing strategy for your real estate business by investing in website development, search engine optimization (SEO), social media marketing, email marketing, online advertising, virtual tours and 3D visualization, as well as online reviews and testimonials. This will increase visibility, engagement, and leads, while also establishing your brand presence and credibility in the competitive real estate market.

Finding Properties

Starting a real estate business takes a good eye for discovering properties that connect with your business goals and meet the demands of your target market. Whether you're looking for residential, commercial, or investment properties, the process of locating them combines market research, networking, and strategic alliances.

Let's get into the exciting process of discovering properties when establishing a real estate business

Market research and analysis:
Conducting extensive market research and analysis is the cornerstone of finding properties for your real estate company. Begin by identifying and analyzing your target market's demographics, tastes, and trends. Analyze local real estate market data, such as property prices, supply and demand trends, rental yields, and vacancy rates. Consider location, neighborhood amenities, schools, transportation, and economic indicators when identifying regions for property investment and development.

Networking and Relationships:

Building contacts and networking with other real estate professionals, property owners, developers, and industry players may lead to important insights and opportunities for property acquisition. Attend real estate networking events, join industry groups, and participate in local community activities to meet potential property suppliers and grow your professional network. Establishing trust and confidence in your network may lead to off-market possibilities, exclusive listings, and recommendations to properties that are not publicly available.

Real Estate Agents and Brokers:

Collaborating with professional real estate agents and brokers who have extensive knowledge of the local market can help you identify properties for your real estate business. Establish contacts with trustworthy agents and brokers that specialize in your desired market or property type. Communicate your particular criteria and investment objectives to them, and then use their knowledge, networks, and access to Multiple Listing Service (MLS) databases to find appropriate properties that match your needs.

Online Property Listings: These platforms and real estate markets make it easy to find homes in various areas and types. Visit prominent real estate websites like Zillow, Realtor.com, Redfin, and LoopNet to explore available homes, examine photographs, verify property data, and filter listings based on your preferences. Set up personalized property alerts to receive notifications when new properties that meet your criteria become available, keeping you up to date on the latest property prospects in your desired market.

Utilize direct marketing and outreach techniques to identify:

Potential property opportunities and engage with interested sellers. Send targeted mailers, postcards, or letters to property owners in your target market, indicating your interest in buying properties and emphasizing the advantages of working with your real estate company. In addition, use internet channels such as social media, email marketing, and networking groups to contact property owners, investors, and landlords to inquire about suitable properties.

Driving and Walking Around:

Sometimes the most successful approach to locate houses is to use traditional tactics such as driving and wandering around areas. Take the time to tour several neighborhoods and places in your chosen market, paying attention to houses that pique your interest. Look for distressed properties, vacant lots, or properties that have the potential to be renovated or redeveloped. Engage with local people, business owners, and property owners to learn more about prospective property possibilities in the region.

Public Records and Auctions:

Public records and property auctions may also help you find possible properties for your real estate firm. To find properties for sale or auction, check public documents such as foreclosure listings, tax liens, and distressed property notices. Attend property auctions held by government agencies, banks, or auction houses to bid on repossessed, bank-owned, or delinquent assets. Prepare to do rigorous due diligence and understand the risks connected with acquiring properties at auction.

Locating properties while establishing a real estate business necessitates a proactive and deliberate strategy that includes market research, networking, using web resources, engaging with real estate experts, and exploring numerous channels for property prospects. By using a combination of these tactics and remaining persistent in your search, you may find properties that meet your investment goals, cater to the needs of your target market, and contribute to the success of your real estate business.

Strategies for Property Acquisition

Acquiring properties is a critical component of launching and expanding a real estate firm. It entails selecting and securing properties that meet your investment goals, whether for residential, business, or investment uses. Strategic planning, market knowledge, negotiation skills, and financial acumen are all necessary for a successful property transaction. Let's look at some of the most appealing ways for acquiring property while establishing a real estate firm.

1. Define the Investment Criteria:

Before you start looking for property, you must first determine your investing requirements and objectives. Determine the sort of property you want to buy (residential, commercial, or multifamily), your preferred location, goal return on investment (ROI), financial limits, and risk tolerance. Clarifying your investment criteria allows you to cut down your search and focus on properties that match your unique needs.

2. Market Research and Analysis:

Conduct in-depth market research and analysis to uncover prospective opportunities and evaluate market circumstances. Analyze local real estate market trends, property prices, supply and demand dynamics, rental yields, and economic data. Assess aspects such as neighborhood growth potential, employment market stability, infrastructure development, and demographic trends to find regions with high investment potential.

3. Network with Industry Professionals:

Networking with real estate professionals, such as agents, brokers, investors, developers, and property managers, may give useful information and prospects for property purchase. Create contacts with specialists that specialize in your target market or property type. Attend networking events, industry associations, and local real estate groups to broaden your network and gain access to off-market possibilities.

4. Use Multiple Acquisition Channels:

Consider a variety of property acquisition methods, such as internet listings, real estate agents, auctions, direct marketing, and referrals. Use internet platforms like MLS listings, real estate websites, and property markets to find available homes. Work with seasoned real estate agents and brokers who have access to unique listings and off-market options. To find possible opportunities, go to property auctions, go through distressed property listings, and use direct marketing tactics.

5. **Off Market Opportunities:**

Off-market properties, often known as pocket listings or private sales, are those that are not openly listed in the market. These possibilities may come as a result of personal contacts, networking, or direct approach to property owners. Building relationships with property owners, investors, and industry professionals can lead to off-market possibilities that may not be available through standard channels. Approach property owners directly or through intermediaries to seek off-market opportunities and negotiate advantageous terms.

6. **Diligence and Financial Analysis:**

Prior to making an acquisition choice, do rigorous due diligence and financial analysis on possible properties. Assess the property's condition, location, market worth, rental income possibilities, costs, and any dangers. Examine financial papers, property inspection reports, title documents, zoning restrictions, and any legal concerns that might impact the property's value or investment possibilities. Conduct financial analysis, including cash flow predictions, ROI calculations, and sensitivity analysis, to determine the property's financial feasibility and investment return.

7. **Negotiation and Offer Submission:**

   When it comes to property acquisition, effective negotiation skills are vital. Create a smart bargaining approach based on your investment goals and current market conditions. Present competing bids that are consistent with the property's market worth, taking into account criteria such as property condition, location, and potential for value increase. Prepare to negotiate terms and circumstances, such as price, financing, closing timeframe, and contingencies, in order to get advantageous purchase terms.

8. **Get Financing and Close the Deal:**

   Once a mutually agreeable agreement has been established, get finance for the property purchase via mortgage lenders, private investors, or alternative financing sources. Work directly with lenders to agree loan conditions, get financing, and finish the closing process. Conduct a final review of all papers, including the purchase agreement, loan agreements, and closing disclosures, to confirm compliance with all applicable legal and regulatory requirements. Close the contract and take possession of the property to complete the buying process.

Property acquisition is a strategic and multifaceted process that includes defining investment criteria, conducting market research, networking with industry professionals, utilizing multiple acquisition channels, investigating off-market opportunities, performing due diligence, negotiating terms, obtaining financing, and closing the deal. Using these tactics and market data, you may find and buy properties that meet your investment goals, contribute to the growth of your real estate firm, and create a positive return on investment.

Conducting Property Due Diligence

Property due diligence is a vital phase in the real estate investment process that entails undertaking extensive research, analysis, and evaluation of a property to determine its possible risks, possibilities, and investment feasibility. Whether you're buying a home for residential, business, or investment purposes, completing thorough due diligence is critical to making educated decisions and reducing any hazards. Let's look at the fascinating process of completing property due diligence while launching a real estate firm.

Research and analysis

Begin by gathering the necessary information and performing thorough research on the property and its surroundings. This entails reviewing property records, zoning restrictions, title papers, tax assessments, and any legal or regulatory issues affecting the property. Investigate the area and market trends to gain a better understanding of elements such as property valuations, rental rates, vacancy rates, and demand drivers.

Physical inspection

Conduct a thorough physical evaluation of the property to determine its condition, structural integrity, and any maintenance or repair needs. Hire a certified home inspector or building contractor to check the whole property, including the exterior, interior, roof, foundation, electrical, plumbing, HVAC systems, and other structural elements. Identify any evident flaws, risks, or inadequacies that may necessitate repair or influence the property's value.

Financial analysis

Conduct a thorough financial analysis to determine the property's investment potential and financial viability. Consider issues including the purchase price, financing alternatives, closing fees, property taxes, insurance premiums, and continuing operational expenditures. To estimate the property's prospective profitability and investment return, use expected rental revenue, cash flow predictions, return on investment (ROI), and other financial measures.

Market Comparable

Examine comparable properties (comps) in the region to determine the property's market worth and price in relation to similar properties. Examine recent sales data, similar property listings, and market trends to evaluate the property's fair market worth and determine if the asking price is appropriate. Consider the size, location, condition, amenities, and recent sales prices of similar properties in the area.

Legal and Regulatory Compliance

Ensure that the property meets all applicable legal and regulatory requirements, such as zoning, building codes, environmental rules, and land use limitations. Examine municipal, planning, and public documents to ensure compliance with zoning restrictions, as well as any existing permits or infractions. Determine any possible legal or regulatory difficulties that may impact the property's usage, occupancy, or development possibilities.

Environmental Assessment

Conduct an environmental assessment of the property to identify any potential environmental hazards or contaminants that could lead to risks or liabilities. Hire a skilled environmental consultant to do a Phase I Environmental Site Assessment (ESA) to determine potential environmental concerns, such as pollution by hazardous chemicals, pollutants, or hazardous waste. If necessary, undertake additional testing or analysis to determine the level of contamination and potential remediation solutions.

Tenancy and Lease Analysis

Thoroughly review the current leases, tenant agreements, and rental history if the property is leased or rented. Examine lease agreements, rental conditions, occupancy rates, and tenant payment histories to determine the consistency of rental revenue and occupancy levels. Examine the quality of existing tenants, lease expiration dates, and any lease conditions or restrictions that might affect the property's cash flow or investment possibilities.

Risk Assessment and Mitigation

Identify and analyze possible hazards to the property, such as physical, financial, legal, and market threats. Determine the probability and potential impact of each risk on the property's value and investment performance. Create strategies and contingency plans to manage identified risks, such as securing insurance coverage, negotiating advantageous purchase terms, dealing with maintenance concerns, or seeking legal counsel to settle any legal or regulatory issues.

Completing property due diligence is a complex and diverse procedure that entails investigating, analyzing, and assessing numerous elements of a property in order to determine its investment potential and mitigate potential hazards. Real estate investors who conduct extensive due diligence may make educated judgments, discover opportunities for value development, and avoid potential hazards when acquiring assets for their real estate businesses.

Negotiating Deals and Contracts for Starting a Real Estate Business

Negotiating deals and contracts is an essential ability for success in the real estate business. Effective negotiation techniques are critical for achieving favorable terms, mitigating risks, and maximizing value in your real estate business, whether you're purchasing properties, securing financing, or finalizing lease agreements.

Let's look at the fascinating art of negotiating transactions and contracts while beginning a real estate business:

Understanding the objectives and priorities: Before getting into talks, it's vital to clearly establish your objectives, priorities, and intended outcomes. Whether you're negotiating a property purchase, finance arrangement, or leasing contract, determine your major goals, such as price, terms, conditions, and timetable. Understand the needs and motivations of the other parties participating in the negotiation to identify common ground and produce mutually beneficial solutions.

Conducting Research and Preparation: Prepare properly for talks by performing research and obtaining pertinent information on the property, market circumstances, comparable sales data, financing choices, and legal factors. Understand the current market trends, property prices, and competitive environment to strengthen your negotiation position and make educated judgments. Anticipate probable objections, concerns, and counterarguments from the opposing party and devise tactics to handle them successfully.

Building Rapport & Relationships: Establishing rapport and creating favorable connections with the other parties participating in the negotiation may encourage open communication, trust, and collaboration. Take the time to listen attentively, grasp the other party's perspective, and display empathy and respect. Building rapport may establish a suitable climate for collaborative communication, innovative problem-solving, and achieving mutually accepted decisions.

Communicating Effectively:

Effective communication is important to effective negotiation. Clearly describe your wants, preferences, and aspirations, using convincing and appealing language to convey your stance. Be forceful yet courteous in communicating your objectives and asking for favorable conditions. Listen attentively to the other party's concerns, ask clarifying questions, and endeavor to grasp their underlying motives and goals.

Seeking Win-Win Solutions:

Strive to negotiate win-win solutions that serve the needs and interests of all parties concerned. Look for opportunities to create value and find creative solutions that satisfy both sides' objectives. Explore alternate solutions and compromises that can benefit all parties while keeping your fundamental objectives. Collaborative negotiating tactics, such as ethical negotiation or interest-based bargaining, can help build collaboration and achieve excellent outcomes for everyone involved.

Managing Emotions and Concessions:

Negotiations may be emotionally stressful, especially when dealing with high-stakes deals or competing interests. Stay composed, calm, and focused during negotiations, avoiding emotional reactions or confrontational behavior. Manage expectations and be prepared to make concessions or compromises when necessary to reach a mutually acceptable agreement. Prioritize your non-negotiables while remaining flexible on less critical issues to facilitate progress and maintain positive relationships.

Documenting Agreements:

Once negotiations are successful, it's essential to document the agreed-upon terms and conditions in a legally binding contract or agreement. Work with legal professionals or real estate attorneys to draft comprehensive contracts that accurately reflect the negotiated terms, rights, and obligations of all parties involved. Review the contract carefully to ensure clarity, completeness, and compliance with applicable laws and regulations before signing.

Following Up and Closing:

After reaching an agreement, follow up promptly to finalize any remaining details, address outstanding issues, and coordinate the closing process. Ensure that all parties fulfill their respective obligations and meet deadlines outlined in the contract. Work closely with relevant stakeholders, such as lenders, inspectors, and attorneys, to facilitate a smooth and timely closing. Celebrate the successful negotiation and closing of the deal, and maintain positive relationships with the other parties for future opportunities.

Negotiating deals and contracts is a vital skill for starting and succeeding in the real estate business. By understanding objectives and priorities, conducting research and preparation, building rapport and relationships, communicating effectively, seeking win-win solutions, managing emotions and concessions, documenting agreements, and following up diligently, real estate professionals can negotiate favorable deals, mitigate risks, and achieve success in the dynamic and competitive real estate industry.

Managing Property

Managing properties is an important part of running a successful real estate firm, whether you're dealing with residential, commercial, or investment properties. Effective property management includes monitoring day-to-day operations, maintaining buildings, managing tenant relationships, and optimizing return on investment.

Let's look at the fascinating art of managing properties while establishing a real estate business:

Property Maintenance and Repair: Ensure that properties are well-kept and in good shape in order to attract and retain renters, protect property value, and reduce maintenance difficulties. Create a proactive maintenance strategy that includes frequent inspections, routine maintenance chores, and quick fixes for any problems that develop. Respond quickly to maintenance requests and solve issues to improve tenant happiness and property value.

Tenant Screening and Leasing: Implement extensive tenant screening methods to find dependable and responsible renters who will pay rent on time, follow lease conditions, and maintain the property appropriately. Conduct background checks, verify employment and income, and review rental history and references. To avoid disagreements and assure compliance, draft thorough lease agreements that clearly define the rights, obligations, and expectations of both renters and landlords.

Rent Collection and Financial Management: Establish effective rent collection systems to secure regular rent payments and positive cash flow for your real estate firm. Implement online payment alternatives, set up automatic reminders, and enforce lease restrictions for rent payments and late fines. Maintain accurate financial records, analyze income and spending, and evaluate property performance in order to determine profitability and make sound financial decisions.

Tenant Relations and Customer Service: Cultivate great connections with renters by offering exceptional customer service, responding quickly to their wants and concerns, and keeping communication open. Respond to tenant queries, maintenance requests, and concerns in a timely and professional way to foster trust and rapport. To ensure tenant satisfaction and retention, politely address tenant complaints and conflicts.

Property Marketing and Vacancy Management: Create effective marketing strategies to recruit and retain renters while reducing vacancy rates in your buildings. Use online listings, social media, property websites, and signage to promote available apartments and attract potential renters. Use tenant retention methods, including lease renewals, incentives, and responsive customer service, to encourage renters to remain longer and decrease turnover.

Compliance and Legal Consideration: Ensure that all applicable laws, regulations, and housing codes govern property management, tenant-landlord interactions, fair housing policies, and safety requirements. Stay up-to-date on local, state, and federal legislation governing rental properties, as well as landlord-tenant rights and duties. Address legal and regulatory requirements for lease agreements, security deposits, eviction processes, and property inspections.

Emergency Planning and Risk Management:

Create thorough emergency preparation plans and practices to handle possible hazards and crises such as natural catastrophes, property damage, and tenant emergencies. Maintain adequate insurance coverage, such as property insurance, liability insurance, and landlord insurance, to secure your assets and limit risk. Install safety features such as smoke detectors, fire extinguishers, and security systems to ensure tenant and property safety.

Professional Growth and Continuous Improvement: Invest in continuous professional development and training to keep up with industry trends, best practices, and technology development in property management. Join professional organizations, attend industry conferences, and take part in educational programs to improve your knowledge and abilities as a property manager. Continuously solicit input from renters, property owners, and industry peers to identify areas for improvement and execute methods to improve property management procedures.

Managing properties while establishing a real estate firm necessitates a deliberate and proactive strategy to ensure property maintenance, tenant satisfaction, and maximum investment returns. Real estate professionals who focus on property maintenance, tenant screening, rent collection, tenant relations, property marketing, compliance, emergency preparedness, and professional development can effectively manage properties, mitigate risks, and succeed in the competitive real estate market.

Setting Up Property Management Systems

Setting up property management systems is an important step in launching a real estate firm because it lays the groundwork for efficient and successful property management. These systems include the tools, methods, and technology needed to handle many areas of property management, such as leasing, rent collection, maintenance, tenant communication, financial administration, and reporting.

Let's take a look at the key components and factors for setting up property management systems

1) Property Management Software: Invest in powerful property management software that streamlines day-to-day operations and centralizes property management tasks. Choose software that offers lease administration, tenant screening, rent collection, maintenance monitoring, financial reporting, and communication options. Look for cloud-based solutions that are scalable, accessible from any device, and integrate with other corporate tools.

2) Tenant Management: Implement tenant management mechanisms, such as onboarding, lease negotiations, rent collection, and communication. Create uniform procedures for screening new renters, confirming income and

references, and signing lease agreements online. Use property management software to automate rent collection, issue rent reminders, and monitor payment history. Establish communication channels to rapidly respond to tenant queries, maintenance requests, and concerns.

3. Maintenance and repair: To keep properties in good shape, establish processes for managing property maintenance and repairs. Create maintenance schedules and processes for routine inspections, preventative maintenance, and emergency repairs. Use property management software to handle maintenance requests, allocate jobs to contractors or in-house maintenance personnel, and track completion progress. For accounting and reporting purposes, set up a system to capture maintenance operations and costs.

4. Financial management: Create financial management systems that cover budgeting, accounting, rent collection, cost monitoring, and financial reporting. Create accounting procedures for documenting rental income, tracking costs, and handling property-related funds. Use property management or accounting software to automate financial operations, produce reports, and monitor key performance indicators, including occupancy rates, rental income, and costs.

5. Lease and Document Management: To ensure legal and regulatory compliance, implement leasing and paperwork management systems. Keep structured records of lease agreements, tenant information, real estate paperwork, insurance policies, and legal documents. Create consistent lease templates and procedures for execution, renewal, and termination. Use document management systems or cloud storage solutions to safely store and manage property-related documents.

6.Tenant Communication and Engagement: Create processes for tenant communication and engagement to promote positive tenant relationships and increase tenant satisfaction. Set up communication channels such as email, phone, and online portals for tenants to submit maintenance requests, pay rent, and contact property management staff. Create a system for responding to tenant requests, resolving issues, and giving timely information on property affairs.

7. Compliance and Legal Consideration: Ensure that property management systems include processes for meeting legal and regulatory requirements for property management, tenant-landlord interactions, fair housing standards, and data privacy. Stay up-to-date on local, state, and federal legislation impacting property management and put in place procedures to

assure lease agreements, evictions, safety, and fair housing compliance.

8. Training and support: Provide property management employees with training and assistance so that they can effectively use property management systems. Provide training programs, workshops, and tools to educate employees on software features, operating processes, customer service standards, and legal needs. Provide continuous support and technical assistance for any difficulties or questions that arise during property management operations.

Finally, building up property management systems entails putting in place tools, procedures, and technologies to streamline property management chores, improve operational efficiency, and provide excellent service to renters and property owners. Real estate organizations may successfully manage properties, reduce risks, and succeed in the competitive real estate market by implementing systems for tenant management, maintenance, financial management, paperwork, communication, compliance, and staff training.

Managing tenant relations and leases

Handling tenant relations and leases is an important part of launching and running a successful real estate firm. Building strong connections with renters and properly managing lease agreements are critical to tenant satisfaction, property retention, and overall business success.

When launching a real estate firm, it's critical to focus on tenant relations by creating a welcoming and professional workplace for them. This starts with open and honest communication from the first engagement with potential renters and continues throughout the lease period. Establishing open lines of communication enables renters to express their issues, ask questions, and give feedback, which fosters trust and teamwork.

Providing excellent customer service is an important component of managing tenant relations. Responding quickly to tenant questions, responding to maintenance requests, and resolving any issues or complaints displays a dedication to tenant satisfaction. Implementing an effective system for managing tenant interactions, whether via phone, email, or an online portal, makes renters feel heard and appreciated.

Furthermore, setting clear expectations and boundaries through lease agreements is critical to sustaining strong tenant relationships. Lease agreements should clearly describe both renters' and landlords' rights and duties, including rent payment conditions, maintenance obligations, occupancy regulations, and lease renewal procedures. Landlords can avoid misunderstandings and problems during the lease period.

In addition to dealing with tenants, correctly managing lease agreements is crucial to the success of any real estate firm. This includes extensive tenant screening to identify dependable and responsible renters who are likely to fulfill their lease responsibilities. Background checks, confirming employment and income, and reviewing rental history may all help discover eligible renters who are a good fit for the property.

Preparing lease agreements that safeguard the landlord's interests while also providing renters with fair and acceptable conditions is critical once tenants have been selected. Lease agreements should include important details, including rent amount, payment due dates, security deposit requirements, maintenance obligations, pet restrictions, and lease renewal choices. Working with legal specialists or real estate attorneys to design detailed lease agreements guarantees that they follow local laws and regulations.

Throughout the lease period, landlords must efficiently manage lease agreements by enforcing lease conditions, collecting rent payments on schedule, and dealing with any lease breaches or disputes that may occur. Implementing a rent collection system, whether through online payments, checks, or direct deposits, ensures that landlords get their rent payments on time and regularly.

Finally, maintaining tenant relationships and leases is an important component of launching and running a real estate firm. Real estate businesses can foster positive tenant relations, minimize disputes, and create a favorable environment for long-term success by prioritizing tenant satisfaction, providing exceptional customer service, establishing clear expectations through lease agreements, and effectively managing lease agreements.

Ensures property maintenance and upkeep

Property maintenance and upkeep are critical when starting a real estate business because they directly impact tenant satisfaction, property value, and overall business success. Effective property maintenance not only preserves the property's physical condition, but it also improves its appeal, attracts quality tenants, and reduces potential issues that may arise over time.

Conducting an in-depth assessment of the property's condition is one of the first steps in ensuring its maintenance. This includes checking both the interior and exterior of the property for signs of wear and tear, damage, or potential hazards. Determine which areas need attention, such as plumbing, electrical systems, HVAC systems, roofing, flooring, and landscaping.

Creating a proactive maintenance plan is critical for staying ahead of maintenance issues and resolving them quickly. Set up a routine for regular inspections and preventive maintenance tasks like servicing HVAC systems, cleaning gutters, inspecting roofing, testing smoke detectors, and maintaining landscaping. Landlords can prevent minor issues from becoming larger, more costly problems by proactively addressing maintenance tasks.

Establishing relationships with trustworthy and qualified contractors and service providers is critical for ensuring timely and efficient property maintenance. Create a network of dependable professionals, such as plumbers, electricians, HVAC technicians, roofers, landscapers, and general contractors, who can handle maintenance issues quickly and effectively. When selecting contractors, conduct thorough due diligence by checking their credentials, references, and insurance coverage to ensure they meet quality standards.

Using technology and software solutions can help streamline property maintenance processes and boost efficiency. Install property management software or maintenance management systems that enable landlords to schedule maintenance tasks, track work orders, communicate with contractors, and monitor maintenance costs. Mobile apps and online portals can help landlords, tenants, and service providers communicate more effectively, resulting in faster response times and improved coordination.

Effective communication with tenants is critical for ensuring property maintenance and promptly responding to maintenance requests. Establish clear channels of communication, such as phone, email, or an online portal, for tenants to submit maintenance requests and report issues. Respond to maintenance requests in a timely manner, and keep tenants informed about the status of repairs or maintenance work. Providing tenants with access to a dedicated maintenance hotline or emergency contact can help resolve urgent maintenance issues outside of regular business hours.

Regularly assessing and improving property maintenance processes is essential for continuous improvement and maintaining property value. Conduct regular reviews of maintenance procedures, solicit feedback from tenants and service providers, and implement changes or adjustments as needed. Stay informed about industry best practices, new technologies, and innovative maintenance solutions to enhance property maintenance practices and stay ahead of evolving trends.

In conclusion, ensuring property maintenance and upkeep is essential for starting and managing a successful real estate business. By developing proactive maintenance plans, establishing relationships with reliable contractors, utilizing technology solutions, communicating effectively with tenants, and continuously improving maintenance processes, real estate businesses can preserve property value, enhance tenant satisfaction, and create a conducive environment for long-term success.

Scaling Your Business

Scaling your real estate business is an exciting yet challenging endeavor that involves expanding operations, increasing revenue, and growing your market presence. Whether you're a seasoned investor or just starting in the industry, scaling your business requires strategic planning, careful execution, and a focus on long-term growth. Let's delve into the captivating journey of scaling your real estate business:

Strategic Planning: Begin by developing a clear vision and strategic plan for scaling your real estate business. Define your goals, objectives, and desired outcomes for expansion, such as increasing the number of properties in your portfolio, expanding into new markets, or diversifying your investment strategies. Conduct a SWOT analysis (Strengths, Weaknesses, Opportunities, and Threats) to assess your current position and identify areas for growth and improvement. Develop a roadmap outlining key milestones, strategies, and action steps for achieving your scaling goals.

Market Research and Analysis: Conduct comprehensive market research and analysis to identify lucrative opportunities for expansion and growth. Explore potential markets, neighborhoods, and property types that align with your investment criteria and growth objectives. Analyze market trends, demographics, rental demand, property values, and economic indicators to assess market viability and identify areas of high growth potential. Leverage data-driven insights to inform your investment decisions and strategic expansion plans.

Financing and Capital: Secure adequate financing and capital to support your scaling efforts. Evaluate various financing options, including traditional bank loans, private equity, crowdfunding, and partnerships, to determine the most suitable financing structure for your business. Create financial projections and cash flow forecasts to assess your funding needs and determine the amount of capital required for scaling. Explore creative financing strategies, such as leveraging existing assets, reinvesting profits, or raising capital from investors, to fund your growth initiatives.

Operational Efficiency: Streamline and optimize your operational processes to enhance efficiency and scalability. Implement scalable systems and technologies, such as property management software, customer relationship management (CRM) systems, and automated workflows, to streamline operations, improve productivity, and scale your business operations. Standardize processes, procedures, and workflows to ensure consistency and scalability across your real estate portfolio. Invest in staff training and development to equip your team with the skills and expertise required to effectively support your scaling efforts.

Diversification and Expansion: To fuel growth and mitigate risk, diversify your real estate portfolio and explore new markets or property types. Consider diversifying your investment strategy by acquiring properties in different geographic locations, asset classes, or investment strategies, such as residential, commercial, multifamily, or mixed-use properties. Explore opportunities for vertical integration or diversification into related real estate sectors, such as property management, development, or real estate services, to create additional revenue streams and enhance your market presence.

Strategic Partnerships and Collaborations: Forge strategic partnerships and collaborations with industry stakeholders, such as real estate agents, property managers, contractors, lenders, and investors, to facilitate growth and expansion. Collaborate with reputable professionals and service providers who can support your scaling efforts with their expertise, resources, and networks. Explore joint ventures, syndications, or strategic alliances with other real estate professionals or investors to pool resources, share risks, and capitalize on mutual opportunities for growth.

Marketing and Branding: Invest in marketing and branding initiatives to increase your visibility, attract new clients, and expand your market reach. Develop a comprehensive marketing strategy that includes online and offline channels, such as digital marketing, social media, networking events, direct mail, and advertising, to promote your real estate services and properties to prospective clients and investors. Build a strong brand identity and reputation in the market by delivering exceptional service, maintaining high ethical standards, and consistently delivering value to your clients.

Monitoring and Evaluation: Continuously monitor and evaluate your scaling efforts to track progress, assess performance, and make data-driven adjustments as needed. Set key performance indicators (KPIs) and metrics to measure the success of your scaling initiatives, such as revenue growth, profit margins, property occupancy rates, return on investment (ROI), and customer satisfaction. Regularly review your strategic plan, financial projections, and operational metrics to identify areas for improvement and refine your scaling strategies for optimal results. Scaling your real estate business requires a strategic and systematic approach that involves careful planning, diligent execution, and a commitment to long-term growth. By focusing on strategic planning, market research, financing, operational efficiency, diversification, strategic partnerships, marketing, and continuous monitoring and evaluation, real estate professionals can successfully scale their businesses and achieve sustainable growth in the dynamic and competitive real estate market.

Growth and Expansion Strategies in the Real Estate Business

Strategic planning, inventive thinking, and aggressive execution are required for real estate firm expansion and growth. Here are detailed tactics for obtaining development and expansion within the real estate industry:

Market analysis and opportunity identification:

Conduct extensive market research and analysis to discover prospective areas for development and expansion. Analyze market trends, demographics, economic indicators, and demand-supply dynamics to identify rising markets, undiscovered niches, and profitable investment prospects. Concentrate on markets with great development potential, robust demand for rental units, and attractive economic circumstances for real estate investment

Diversifying the investment portfolio:

Diversify your investing portfolio by experimenting with different property kinds, asset classes, and geographical areas. Consider investing in residential, commercial, multifamily, mixed-use, or industrial properties to diversify risk and provide many revenue sources. Look for chances in both established and new markets to achieve balanced growth and reduce susceptibility to market changes.

3. Property acquisition and development:

Seek out smart purchase and development options to broaden your real estate portfolio and boost asset value. Identify undervalued or distressed buildings with the potential to create greater profits through renovation, redevelopment, or repositioning. Seek out properties with value-add potential, such as those in emerging communities, underutilized space, or zoning possibilities for redevelopment.

Strategic Partnerships and Collaborations:

Form strategic alliances and collaborations with industry players such as real estate developers, property managers, investors, lenders, and service providers to promote development and expansion. Collaborate with respected specialists who can offer experience, resources, and networks to help you with your expansion plans. Consider joint ventures, syndications, or strategic partnerships to pool resources, share risks, and capitalize on mutually beneficial development prospects.

6. Technology adoption and innovation:

Embrace technology and innovation to increase operational efficiency, optimize procedures, and make better decisions in your real estate firm. Use property management software, customer relationship management (CRM) systems, financial analytics tools, and other technology solutions to automate operations, optimize resource allocation, and obtain insights into market trends and performance measures. Use new technologies like AI, VR, and block-chain to transform property management, marketing, and transaction procedures.

7. Scaling operational capability:

To support growth and development, increase your operational skills by investing in infrastructure, systems, and personnel. Expand your property management operations by recruiting experienced property managers, leasing agents, maintenance technicians, and administrative personnel to handle growing property volume and tenant interactions. Implement scalable systems, procedures, and workflows that simplify operations, boost productivity, and improve customer service. Invest in personnel training and development to ensure that your team has the skills and knowledge required to effectively support your growth plans.

8. Capital Deployment and Financing Strategy:

Create effective capital deployment and financing methods to support your development and expansion plans. To generate funds for property acquisitions, development projects, or portfolio growth, consider several financing methods such as standard bank loans, private equity, mezzanine financing, crowdsourcing, and syndication. To determine the best financing structure for your company, consider the cost of capital as well as the terms and conditions of each option. Create financial forecasts and investment models to assess the viability and potential returns of growth projects and make sound funding decisions.

9. Branding and marketing:

Invest in brand development and marketing strategies to boost awareness, attract customers, and broaden your market reach. Create a compelling brand identity and value proposition that appeals to your target audience and differentiates you from the competition. Promote your real estate services and properties with complete marketing tactics that include digital marketing, social media, content marketing, networking events, and targeted advertising. Showcase your track record, experience, and success stories to gain credibility and confidence from clients and investors.

10. Adapting to market trends and dynamics:

Stay nimble and adaptable to changing market trends, customer tastes, and industry dynamics in order to capitalize on opportunities and reduce risks. Keep track of market circumstances, legislative changes, technological breakthroughs, and demographic shifts that might affect real estate markets and investment strategies. Anticipate future trends and disruptions in the real estate market, such as demographic shifts, urbanization, sustainability, and technological innovation, and position your company to benefit from new possibilities while remaining competitive.

11. Continuous Monitoring and Evaluation:

Continuously monitor and analyze the success of your development and expansion projects to track progress, assess results, and make data-driven changes as appropriate. Establish key performance indicators (KPIs) and metrics to assess the effectiveness of your expansion strategy, such as revenue growth, profit margins, return on investment (ROI), occupancy rates, customer satisfaction, and market share. Regularly examine your strategic strategy, financial predictions, and operational KPIs to discover areas for improvement and fine-tune your growth tactics for the best outcomes.

Establishing comprehensive development and expansion plans is critical for long-term success and sustainability in the real estate business. Real estate professionals can achieve significant growth and expansion while navigating the complexities of the ever-changing real estate market by leveraging market opportunities, diversifying their investment portfolio, forming strategic partnerships, embracing technology and innovation, scaling operational capabilities, effectively deploying capital, building a strong brand, remaining adaptable to market dynamics, and monitoring performance.

Scaling operations efficiently

Scaling operations efficiently is an important part of launching and expanding a real estate firm. As your company grows, you must improve your operational procedures, simplify workflows, and boost efficiency in order to meet greater demand, manage larger portfolios, and provide superior service to customers. Let's look at complete ideas for growing operations efficiently in the real estate market.

1. Standardizing procedures and workflows:

Standardize operational procedures and workflows across all areas of your real estate firm, such as property management, leasing, maintenance, financial management, and customer service. Create standard templates, checklists, and processes for common tasks, including tenant screening, lease administration, property upkeep, and financial reporting. Standardizing operations ensures consistency, reduces mistakes, and increases efficiency as your organization grows.

2. Implementing scalable systems and technologies:

Invest in scalable systems and technologies that will automate repetitive procedures, streamline operations, and boost productivity. Implement property management software, CRM systems, accounting software, and other technology solutions to consolidate data, automate procedures, and improve team communication and cooperation. Utilize cloud-based solutions that provide scalability, flexibility, and access from anywhere, allowing your team to manage operations effectively and securely.

3. Staff and Resource Allocation:

Optimize your workforce and resource allocation to meet increasing operational needs as your company grows. Hire extra employees, contractors, or virtual assistants to handle increased workloads and assure timely service delivery. Assess task allocation and adjust worker numbers as needed to avoid burnout, maintain productivity, and achieve service level agreements (SLAs). Provide continual training and professional development opportunities to ensure that your workforce has the skills and information they need to succeed in their professions.

4. Outsource non-core functions:

Consider outsourcing non-core company processes and duties, such as accounting, IT support, marketing, and administration. Outsourcing enables you to tap into specialized expertise, cut overhead expenses, and focus your own resources on vital operations that generate revenue and growth. Collaborate with reliable outsourcing companies or freelancers who can provide high-quality services and help you achieve your company goals.

5. Develop Key Performance Indicators (KPIs):

Establish key performance indicators (KPIs) and metrics to assess the effectiveness and efficiency of your operational procedures. Identify key performance indicators (KPIs) for several aspects of your real estate firm, such as occupancy rates, lease renewal rates, tenant satisfaction, maintenance response times, financial performance measures, and staff productivity. Track and evaluate KPIs on a regular basis to discover areas for improvement, monitor progress toward company objectives, and make data-driven choices to enhance operations.

6. Continuous process improvement:

Encourage feedback, creativity, and cooperation among team members to help your firm foster a culture of continuous process improvement. Regularly collect feedback from employees, renters, and other stakeholders to discover pain areas, inefficiencies, and possibilities for improvement in your operating procedures. Use a structured strategy, such as Lean Six Sigma or Kaizen, to identify, evaluate, and fix process inefficiencies and bottlenecks in order to promote continuous improvement and increase operational efficiency.

7. Scalable Customer Service Strategies:

As your company grows, create a scalable customer service strategy to ensure high levels of service quality and customer happiness. Implement many contact channels, such as phone, email, live chat, and self-service portals, to give customers and renters fast and tailored help. Invest in educating your customer service personnel to manage more queries, address issues quickly, and provide outstanding service experiences that enhance customer loyalty and retention.

8. Risk Management and Compliance:

As your organization grows, strengthen your risk management and compliance policies to reduce operational risks and assure regulatory compliance. Create effective risk management policies and processes to detect, analyze, and reduce risks related to property management, leasing, maintenance, financial management, and legal obligations. Stay up-to-date on current laws, regulations, and industry best practices regulating real estate operations, and take steps to assure compliance in all parts of your organization.

Increasing operations efficiently in a real estate organization necessitates a deliberate and proactive strategy that optimizes processes, leverages technology, effectively allocates resources, measures performance, drives continuous improvement, delivers outstanding customer service, and manages risks. Real estate professionals may successfully manage expansion, improve operational performance, and achieve long-term success in a dynamic and competitive market context by applying complete strategies for efficient scaling.

Managing risks and challenges

Managing risks and obstacles is an important part of launching and running a successful real estate business. The real estate sector is naturally complicated and dynamic, with several risks and obstacles that can affect corporate operations, financial performance, and overall profitability. Managing these risks and obstacles requires meticulous preparation, proactive action, and smart decision-making.

Let's have a thorough talk on handling risks and problems while establishing a real estate business:

1. Market Risks: The real estate market is susceptible to supply and demand variations, economic situations, interest rate changes, and market cycles. Market risks have an impact on property valuations, rental revenue, occupancy rates, and investment returns. Mitigating market risks entails conducting extensive market research and analysis to discover trends, assess market conditions, and make sound investment decisions. Diversifying your real estate portfolio across markets and property types can help reduce risk and exposure to market swings.

2. Financial Risk: Financial hazards in real estate include financing, liquidity, cash flow volatility, and leverage risks. Financial risk mitigation requires securing suitable funding, keeping enough liquidity buffers, and successfully managing cash flow. Financial due diligence, stress testing financial models, and maintaining conservative leverage ratios can all help mitigate financial risks and assure financial stability in unfavorable market situations.

3. **Operational Risk:** Internal variables such as inefficient procedures, an inadequate workforce, poor property management, maintenance difficulties, and legal compliance all contribute to operational hazards. Implementing strong operational processes, investing in technology and automation, and recruiting competent employees are all critical for managing operational risks. Developing detailed risk management policies and processes, conducting frequent property inspections, and adhering to regulatory standards may all help reduce operational risks and guarantee smooth corporate operations.

4. Legal and regulatory risks:

Real estate transactions are subject to a variety of legal and regulatory obligations, such as zoning rules, construction codes, landlord-tenant laws, environmental restrictions, and fair housing legislation. Noncompliance with legal and regulatory obligations can lead to penalties, litigation, and reputational harm. Reduce legal and regulatory risks by educating yourself about applicable laws and regulations, obtaining legal assistance as needed, and strictly adhering to all relevant rules.

5. Reputational Risk:

Poor customer service, ethical failures, unwanted publicity, and conflicts of interest can all put a company's reputation in jeopardy. Protecting your reputation as a real estate professional is critical for establishing confidence and credibility with clients, tenants, and other industry stakeholders. Exceptional customer service, strong ethical standards, and open communication are critical for controlling reputational concerns. Responding quickly to consumer feedback, properly handling complaints, and professionally resolving difficulties may all help safeguard and improve your market image.

6. **Environmental and sustainability risks**: Environmental hazards, such as contaminants, natural catastrophes, and climate change, can have an influence on property values and business operations. Assessing environmental hazards, conducting property due diligence, and implementing environmental management practices are all critical steps in risk mitigation. Adopting sustainability initiatives, such as energy-efficient improvements, green building certifications, and sustainable landscaping, may increase property value, save running costs, and minimize environmental risk.

7. Cybersecurity risks: In today's digital era, real estate enterprises face major cybersecurity threats such as data breaches, cyberattacks, and ransomware. Strong cybersecurity solutions, including encryption, firewalls, antivirus software, and frequent data backups, are critical for safeguarding sensitive information and reducing cybersecurity threats. Training employees on cybersecurity best practices, implementing strong password restrictions, and remaining watchful against phishing attempts may all help you avoid security breaches and protect your company's data.

8. Real estate professionals must be prepared for rising risks and challenges, including technological upheavals, geopolitical instability, and global pandemics. Anticipating and planning for future risks requires staying current on industry developments, monitoring macroeconomic data, and devising contingency plans to manage potential hazards. Building resilience and adaptability into your company's operations, diversifying your investment portfolio, and adopting a conservative financial strategy may all help limit rising risks and assure business continuity during unpredictable times.

Risk and challenge management is a multidimensional process in the real estate business that necessitates proactive measures, strategic planning, and ongoing monitoring. Real estate professionals who identify potential risks, implement appropriate risk management strategies, and remain agile in response to changing market conditions can effectively navigate challenges and position their businesses for long-term success in a dynamic and competitive market environment.

Managing Legal and Ethical Issues

Navigating legal and ethical concerns is critical when launching a real estate firm, as the industry operates under a complicated regulatory framework and needs high ethical standards. Understanding and adhering to legal standards, as well as preserving ethical values, is critical for establishing trust with clients, safeguarding your reputation, and guaranteeing long-term success in the real estate market.

1. **Legal considerations:** Understanding the numerous laws, regulations, and contractual duties that govern property transactions and company operations is essential for navigating the real estate legal environment. Important legal issues for launching a real estate firm include:

License Requirements: Many jurisdictions require real estate professionals to get a license before practicing. Familiarize yourself with your area's license regulations and verify that you are operating lawfully.

Contract Law: Contracts control real estate transactions, such as buy, lease, and listing agreements. Understand the legal ramifications of these contracts, such as their terms and conditions, duties, and breach-of-contract remedies.

Property Law: Familiarize yourself with property rules, such as zoning, land use limits, and ownership rights. When acquiring or developing property, ensure that you follow local zoning rules.

Fair Housing Laws: Follow fair housing rules, which ban discrimination based on race, color, religion, gender, handicap, familial status, or national origin. Avoid using discriminatory techniques in advertising, tenant screening, and property management.

Disclosure Requirements: As required by law, disclose material information and faults regarding properties to prospective purchasers and tenants. Failure to provide important information may result in legal action for misrepresentation.
Environmental restrictions: Think about environmental restrictions that might affect property development and management, such as environmental evaluations, hazardous materials, and wetland protections.

2. Ethical Consideration: Maintaining strong ethical standards is critical for establishing credibility, cultivating client confidence, and preserving the integrity of the real estate business.

When starting a real estate firm, consider the following ethical issues:

Honesty and integrity: Maintain honesty, integrity, and openness in all interactions with clients, customers, and industry stakeholders. Avoid misrepresenting, exaggerating, or concealing crucial information.

Conflict of Interests: Disclose any potential conflicts of interest in deals, such as dual agency or personal financial interests in properties. Act in your clients' best interests and avoid situations where personal interests conflict with fiduciary obligations.

Confidentiality: Maintain client confidentiality and secure any sensitive information collected during transactions. Protect customer privacy, and do not disclose personal information without proper authority.

Professionalism: Maintain professionalism during all interactions with clients, coworkers, and industry professionals. Maintain a professional manner, follow ethical norms of behavior, and treat others with respect and consideration.

Client Representation: During discussions, carefully represent clients and argue for their interests while preserving impartiality and fairness. Provide clients with accurate and unbiased information so they may make educated decisions.

Compliance with Ethical Codes: Follow ethical norms of behavior set by professional organizations, such as the National Association of Realtors' (NAR) Code of Ethics. Familiarize yourself with ethical rules and commit to maintaining high ethical standards in your real estate profession.

3. Risk Management:

Implementing good risk management methods is critical for reducing legal and ethical hazards in your real estate firm. Create risk management rules and processes to discover, analyze, and reduce possible legal and ethical hazards. Employees should receive continual training and instruction on legal and ethical issues, including compliance with laws and ethical standards of behavior. Establish internal controls and supervision procedures to ensure that legal and ethical standards are followed and that any breaches are addressed swiftly.

Ensuring compliance with real estate laws and regulations.

Starting a real estate firm requires navigating legal and ethical problems. The real estate sector operates under a complex set of rules, regulations, and ethical standards that are intended to protect customers, assure fair and transparent transactions, and maintain professional integrity. Understanding and adhering to these legal and ethical standards is critical for real estate entrepreneurs in terms of gaining customer confidence, reducing risks, and laying a firm basis for their businesses.

Compliance with real estate laws and regulations: Real estate professionals must follow a slew of federal, state, and municipal rules and regulations controlling all elements of real estate transactions, property management, and brokerage operations. These laws address issues such as fair housing, anti-discrimination, landlord-tenant relationships, property disclosures, licensing regulations, advertising practices, escrow processes, and consumer protection. Ensuring compliance with these regulations is non-negotiable, and it necessitates continual education, training, and monitoring to keep up with regulatory changes.

2. **License and Certification:** Depending on the jurisdiction, real estate professionals may need to get a license or certification before practicing lawfully. Licensing criteria vary by state but often include completing a pre-licensing study, passing a licensure test, and meeting ongoing education requirements. To prevent any legal consequences, you must be aware of the unique licensing requirements in your region and verify compliance.

3. **Ethics and Professional Conduct:** The real estate profession's essential principles include maintaining ethical standards and engaging in professional conduct. Real estate professionals must adhere to ethical codes of conduct set by industry organizations like the National Association of Realtors (NAR) and uphold the principles of honesty, integrity, transparency, and fiduciary duty in their interactions with clients, customers, and colleagues. The profession's integrity is defined by key ethical duties such as acting in the best interests of clients, maintaining confidentiality, avoiding conflicts of interest, and revealing significant information.

4. **Disclosures and Transparency:** Transparency and complete disclosure are critical concepts in real estate transactions that promote informed decision-making by all parties involved. Real estate professionals are required by law and ethics to disclose important facts and information that may impact a property's value or desirability to prospective purchasers or tenants. This includes

disclosures on property flaws, environmental dangers, zoning restrictions, liens, easements, and any other relevant information that may affect the transaction.

Fair Housing and Anti-Discrimination Laws:

Fair housing rules prohibit housing discrimination based on protected factors such as race, color, national origin, religion, gender, familial status, and disability. Real estate agents must follow fair housing legislation and take proactive steps to provide equal access to housing options for all people. This includes not using discriminatory techniques while promoting, presenting homes, screening renters, or negotiating agreements.

Contract obligations and agreements: Purchase agreements, leasing agreements, listing agreements, and agency agreements are all examples of contractual and legal instruments used in real estate transactions. Understanding the terms and duties specified in these contracts is critical for safeguarding your interests and complying with contractual requirements. Real estate experts are responsible for appropriately interpreting contract provisions, explaining contractual rights and duties to clients, and facilitating the implementation of legally binding agreements.

Risk and Liability Protection: Real estate professionals must prioritize risk mitigation and liability protection. This involves putting in place risk management procedures to detect, analyze, and mitigate potential transaction risks such as property flaws, title concerns, financing contingencies, and legal conflicts. Maintaining proper errors and omissions (E&O) insurance coverage, executing rigorous due diligence procedures, and getting legal assistance as needed can help reduce exposure to liability and protect against any legal claims.

Professional Development and Continuous Education: Real estate rules, regulations, and ethical standards are all subject to change; thus, real estate professionals must engage in continual professional development and continuing education to stay educated and up-to-date on industry trends. Participating in appropriate training programs, taking continuing education courses, and being involved with industry groups and professional networks are all critical for improving knowledge, skills, and compliance with legal and ethical norms.

Managing legal and ethical concerns is an essential component of launching and running a successful real estate firm. Real estate entrepreneurs can lay a solid foundation for their business by prioritizing compliance with real estate laws and regulations, adhering to ethical standards and professional conduct, practicing transparency and disclosure, and investing in ongoing education and professional development.

Ethical Conduct in Real Estate Transactions

Ethical methods in real estate transactions are critical for maintaining integrity, establishing confidence with clients, and keeping industry standards. Real estate agents have a fiduciary obligation to work in their customers' best interests and conduct business with honesty, openness, and fairness.

Here's a full look into ethical procedures in real estate transactions:

Real estate agents have a fiduciary obligation to put their customers' interests over their own and operate in good faith at all times. This obligation involves communicating in an honest and transparent manner, revealing all material information about a property, and fighting for their clients' best interests during the transaction.

Honesty and Integrity: Real estate professionals must be honest and ethical in all their transactions. This involves giving accurate information about properties, market circumstances, and transaction procedures. Misrepresentation or concealing vital information from clients is unethical and can result in legal consequences.

3. Confidentiality: Real estate agents must safeguard client confidentiality and protect sensitive information supplied during transactions. This involves keeping private information about their customers' finances, motives, and personal circumstances discreet unless necessary by law or with the client's permission.

4. Avoiding Conflicts of Interest: Real estate agents must avoid conflicts of interest, which may jeopardize their ability to act in their customers' best interests. This includes abstaining from representing both the buyer and seller in the same transaction (dual agency), unless both parties provide full information and informed consent. Agents should also declare any personal or financial ties that may affect their recommendations to customers.

5. Fair and equal treatment: Real estate professionals must treat all parties involved in a transaction fairly and equitably, regardless of race, ethnicity, religion, gender, sexual orientation, or other protected characteristics. Fair housing rules ban discriminatory tactics in housing transactions, and real estate brokers must follow them to guarantee that everyone has equal access to housing

possibilities.

6. Transparency in Communication: Effective communication is vital in real estate transactions, as is openness, in order to create client confidence. Real estate agents should provide customers with clear and accurate information regarding property listings, prices, market trends, and transaction processes so that they may make educated judgments. They should also quickly report any conflicts of interest or modifications to the transaction.

7. Compliance with Laws and Regulations: Real estate professionals must follow all applicable laws, regulations, and ethical standards when conducting real estate transactions. This involves complying with licensing regulations, fair housing legislation, agency rules, disclosure standards, and other legal duties. Maintaining ethical behavior requires being up-to-date on changes in laws and regulations, as well as receiving advice from legal specialists as necessary.

8. Real estate agents must keep up-to-date on industry trends, best practices, and ethical standards through ongoing professional development and education. Participating in continuing education, training programs, and professional development opportunities enables agents to improve their knowledge and abilities, keep

current on industry developments, and maintain high ethical standards in their work.

The ethical procedures in real estate transactions are critical to promoting trust, integrity, and professionalism within the sector. Real estate professionals may preserve the trust and confidence of their customers and stakeholders by adhering to ethical values such as honesty, openness, confidentiality, fairness, and compliance with laws and regulations.

Dealing With Disputes And Legal Issues.

Handling conflicts and legal concerns is an unavoidable part of running a real estate firm. Disputes and legal problems can develop at any step of a transaction, including contract negotiations, property management, and beyond. Effective conflict and problem management necessitates a combination of proactive measures, clear communication, and creative resolution tactics. Let's look at a thorough method for dealing with conflicts and legal concerns in the real estate market.

1. Prevention with Due Diligence:

The best method to deal with conflicts and legal concerns is to prevent them from happening in the first place. Conducting rigorous due diligence on properties, contracts, and transaction parties can help detect possible dangers and red flags at an early stage. This involves validating property titles, doing inspections, analyzing legal paperwork, and determining the financial sustainability of deals. By addressing any difficulties beforehand, you may reduce the possibility of disagreements later in the process.

2. Clear Communication and Documentation:

Clear and efficient communication is essential for preventing misunderstandings and settling issues peacefully. Real estate professionals should communicate openly with all parties involved in a transaction, such as customers, buyers, sellers, renters, and other stakeholders. Documenting all contacts, agreements, and decisions in writing can help avoid conflicts and offer a comprehensive record of transaction history if they do emerge.

3. Mediation and Alternative Dispute Resolution (ADR):

When issues arise, consider employing mediation or other kinds of alternative dispute resolution (ADR) to settle them outside of court. Mediation entails a neutral third party encouraging conversations between the parties in order to help them find a mutually accepted conclusion. ADR procedures like arbitration or negotiation can be speedier, less expensive, and less confrontational than traditional litigation, making them appealing choices for resolving issues quickly and efficiently.

4. Legal and Expert Advice:

In more complicated or contentious conflicts, legal counsel and professional assistance are required. Real estate professionals should have access to qualified attorneys who can advise and represent them in legal problems. Legal advice may assist in determining the merits of a case, navigating complicated legal issues, negotiating settlements, and representing your interests in court if required.

5. **Compliance with laws and regulations:** Compliance with all applicable laws, regulations, and industry standards is critical for avoiding legal complications and conflicts. Real estate professionals must remain up-to-date on changes to the rules and regulations that regulate real estate transactions, property management, and agency relationships. Compliance with fair housing regulations, anti-discrimination legislation, licensing requirements, and disclosure duties is critical for avoiding legal traps and minimizing potential liabilities.

6. **Documentation and Record-Keeping:**

Effective legal defense and dispute resolution need thorough documentation and record-keeping. Real estate professionals must keep accurate records of all transaction-related papers, conversations, agreements, and disclosures. This includes preserving copies of contracts, property disclosures, inspection reports, communications, and any other documents that may be required to back up your position in the event of a disagreement.

7. **Professionalism and ethical behavior:** Maintaining professionalism and ethical behavior in all transactions is critical for establishing confidence with clients and coworkers while avoiding legal concerns. Real estate professionals should follow ethical standards set by industry groups and regulatory agencies, such as the National Association of Realtors' (NAR) Code of Ethics. Acting in good faith, treating all parties fairly and honestly, and adhering to fiduciary obligations are fundamental elements of ethical behavior in the real estate sector.

8. **Continuous Learning and Adaptation:** The real estate market is always changing, and real estate professionals must keep current on emerging trends, legal changes, and best practices. Continuous learning and professional growth are critical for responding to changing market situations, legislation, and customer preferences. Real estate professionals who are educated and proactive may reduce legal risks, handle conflicts efficiently, and protect their businesses from potential liabilities. Resolving conflicts and legal concerns in the real estate market necessitates a proactive, smart, and professional strategy. Real estate professionals can successfully handle legal difficulties and safeguard their businesses by stressing prevention through due diligence, clear communication and documentation, obtaining expert assistance when necessary, and adhering to ethical and legal norms.

Thriving in the Real Estate Industry

A simple grasp of property transactions is insufficient for success in the real estate market. It necessitates a comprehensive strategy that includes strategic planning, lifelong learning, flexibility, and a dedication to excellence. As you embark on the adventure of starting a real estate firm, it is critical to cultivate a mentality oriented toward not only surviving but flourishing in this dynamic and competitive sector.

1. **Embrace lifelong learning:** The real estate sector is always changing, impacted by market trends, technological breakthroughs, regulatory changes, and increasing customer preferences. To succeed in this environment, it is critical to embrace an attitude of continual learning and professional growth. Stay current with industry news, attend seminars, workshops, and conferences, pursue relevant certifications, and seek out mentors who can provide advice and insights based on their expertise.

2. **Grow a Strong Network:** Building and maintaining a strong professional network is critical to success in the real

estate business. Surround yourself with other industry experts, such as real estate agents, brokers, bankers, lawyers, contractors, and investors. Networking allows for cooperation, recommendations, and access to useful resources and information. Attend networking events, join industry associations, and participate in online forums and social media groups to broaden your network and develop important contacts.

3. **Provide excellent customer service:** Exceptional customer service is essential for success in the real estate industry. Throughout the transaction process, strive to surpass the clients' expectations by delivering customized attention, timely communication, and professional counsel. Understand your customers' needs, address their issues, and exceed expectations to ensure a positive experience. Building a reputation for exceptional service will not only result in return business and recommendations, but it will also contribute to the industry's long-term prosperity.

4. **Take a solution-oriented approach:** There will always be hurdles and obstacles in the real estate sector. Instead of perceiving them as setbacks, look at them as chances to discover innovative solutions and give value to your

clients. A proactive and solution-oriented approach is essential while negotiating a difficult transaction, settling disagreements, or dealing with market changes. Focus on recognizing and meeting your clients' demands, and show that you can manage complexity with professionalism and knowledge.

5. **Stay Tech-Savvy:** Technology plays an important part in modern real estate transactions, from property marketing to virtual tours and client relationship management. Utilize digital tools and platforms to improve corporate processes, increase productivity, and stay ahead of the competition by embracing technology. To remain tech-savvy and relevant in today's digital world, invest in user-friendly real estate software, employ social media and digital marketing methods, and study upcoming technologies such as virtual reality and artificial intelligence.

6. **Identify your brand:** In a competitive market, it's critical to distinguish yourself and your real estate company from your competitors. Determine your unique value proposition and successfully explain it to your target audience. Whether it's specialist experience in a certain area, a tailored approach to client service, or new marketing

methods, emphasize what distinguishes you and why clients should choose to work with you. Creating a distinct brand identity can help you stand out and attract customers who share your beliefs and products.

7. Maintain Financial Discipline: Financial management is critical to long-term success in the real estate market. Create a comprehensive financial strategy that involves proper budgeting, forecasting, and cash flow management. Monitor your spending, keep accurate records of your income and expenses, and have enough money on hand to weather unexpected obstacles or market downturns. Maintain financial discipline, prevent overleveraging, and base investment decisions on careful research and risk assessment.

8. Embrace adaptability and resilience: The real estate sector is naturally cyclical, with phases of expansion and decline. To flourish in this environment, you must embrace adaptation and resilience. Prepare to pivot your strategy, adapt to shifting market conditions, and innovate in response to emerging trends. Maintain agility, be open to new chances, and learn from setbacks and disappointments. Develop a resilient, persevering, and determined mentality

to overcome challenges and achieve long-term success in the real estate sector.

Success in the real estate sector necessitates a comprehensive strategy that incorporates continual learning, networking, great customer service, solution-oriented thinking, technology competence, brand distinction, financial discipline, and adaptability. By following these ideas and techniques, you can position yourself for success and create a profitable real estate firm that will withstand the test of time in a competitive market.

Keeping Up With Market Trends

Keeping up with market trends is critical for success in the real estate sector because it allows professionals to make educated judgments, anticipate changes, and adjust their strategy appropriately. Here are measures to properly remain current on market trends:

1. Continuous monitoring:

Regularly monitor real estate market indicators like property prices, inventory levels, sales volume, and days on market. Keep track of macroeconomic indicators such as interest rates, employment, GDP growth, and inflation, as they all have an impact on overall market conditions.

2. Industry reports and publications:

Subscribe to industry papers, publications, and research studies from credible sources, including real estate organizations, market research firms, and financial institutions. These papers frequently provide insights into market trends, predictions, and potential opportunities or difficulties.

3. Attend industry events and seminars: Attend real estate conferences, seminars, workshops, and networking events where industry professionals offer insights, analysis, and forecasts about market trends. Engage in discussions with colleagues to share ideas and thoughts on current market trends.

4. Use online resources:

Use internet resources such as industry websites, blogs, forums, and social media platforms that cover real estate news and trends. Follow notable real estate experts, economists, and analysts on social media to receive immediate information and expert analysis on market changes.

5. Local Market Insights:

Network with local real estate professionals, attend local organization meetings, and engage with community leaders to learn more about local market trends. Keep up with local zoning restrictions, development projects, infrastructural efforts, and population trends that affect market dynamics.

6. Data analysis and market research:

Analyze historical data using data analytics tools and market research platforms to uncover patterns or trends in property valuations, rental rates, and market demand. Use data-driven insights to make sound investment decisions, pricing strategies, and market positioning.

7. **Customer feedback and market intelligence:** Solicit input from clients, renters, and industry stakeholders to learn about market preferences, new trends, and shifting consumer behavior. Stay tuned to client requirements and preferences in order to predict market movements and adjust your services or offers accordingly.

8. **Stay Updated on Regulatory Changes:**
Stay informed on regulatory changes, policy updates, and legislative developments that may affect the real estate industry. Stay up-to-date on changes in zoning laws, building rules, tax policies, and environmental restrictions that may impact property values, development projects, or investment possibilities.

9. **Interact with Economic Indicators:** Consumer confidence, home affordability, mortgage rates, and employment growth are all important indications of the real estate market's overall health. Pay attention to leading signs that indicate prospective market shifts and modify your plans accordingly.

10. **Professional Growth and Education:** Invest in continuous professional development and education to keep up with market developments, industry best practices, and regulatory changes. Industry groups, educational institutions, and professional development organizations all provide

continuing education courses, webinars, and training programs.

Real estate professionals may obtain a competitive advantage, recognize opportunities, and efficiently handle market hurdles in a fast-changing industry landscape by following these steps and taking a proactive approach to staying current on market trends.

Networking and developing industry relationships.

Networking and cultivating industry contacts are critical components of success in real estate. Establishing strong connections with other professionals, industry experts, and potential clients may lead to new possibilities, give significant insights, and improve your industry reputation.

Here's how to properly network and establish industry relationships:

1. Attending Industry Events: Attend real estate conferences, seminars, trade exhibits, and networking events to meet and interact with fellow industry experts. These events provide an opportunity to network, share ideas, and remain current on industry trends and advancements.

2. Join professional associations: Join appropriate professional societies and organizations in the real estate sector, such as the National Association of Realtors (NAR), local real estate boards, or industry-specific clubs. Membership provides access to networking events, educational materials, industry news, and the opportunity to interact with other professionals in the field.

3. Utilize social media: Use social media networks like LinkedIn, Twitter, and Facebook to build your professional network and connect with industry colleagues. Join real estate-related clubs and communities, engage in discussions, exchange thoughts and materials, and network with other professionals in your sector.

4. Attend local networking events: Attend local real estate networking events, meetings, and mixers hosted by industry associations, investor clubs, or community organizations. These events allow you to network with local experts, create contacts with future clients, and remain current on local market trends.

5. Interact with colleagues and peers: Develop relationships with coworkers, peers, and other real estate professionals at your brokerage business or office. Take the initiative to work on projects together, share recommendations, and communicate knowledge and thoughts. Developing a helpful peer network can help you advance your career and give you new chances.

6. Provide value and expertise: Establish yourself as a useful resource in your field by sharing your skills, thoughts, and information with others. Offer to speak at industry events, publish articles or blog entries on relevant issues, or organize informative webinars or seminars. Providing great material and knowledge

may help you establish a reputation and attract new clients and colleagues.

7. Follow up and stay connected: After meeting new people or attending networking events, send individual texts or emails to convey your gratitude and propose prospects for future cooperation or conversation. Maintain contact with your network by regularly reaching out, sharing important information or resources, and offering support or assistance as needed.

8. Be authentic and genuine: Authenticity and authenticity are essential for developing lasting connections in the real estate market. Maintain sincerity in your conversations, actively listen to others, and express real interest in their job and hobbies. Building trust and rapport with people can strengthen your bonds and result in more successful long-term relationships.

9. Invest in relationship building: Building great industry relationships requires time and work, so invest in cultivating and keeping your ties for the long run. Schedule frequent check-ins, meetings, or coffee conversations with essential connections, and make relationship-building activities a top priority in your professional growth strategy.

Send and receive referrals: Create a trusted professional network, including mortgage brokers, attorneys, contractors, and house inspectors, to whom you can confidently send clients. Similarly, be willing to accept referrals from people in your network and respond whenever possible. Building a referral network can provide reciprocal advantages and build industry ties.

Real estate professionals who actively network and cultivate industry contacts may broaden their professional network, gain valuable insights and opportunities, and position themselves as trusted industry experts. Building solid relationships takes time and effort, but the advantages of having a strong network are vital for long-term success in the real estate industry.

Continuous Education and Professional Development

Continuing education and professional development are critical for real estate professionals to remain competitive, improve their abilities, and adapt to the changing needs of the market. In a dynamic industry like real estate, where market trends, rules, and technology are continuously evolving, continuous learning is critical for staying relevant and succeeding. Here's why continuing education and professional development are so important in the real estate industry:

1. **Keeping up with industry trends:** Continuing education allows real estate professionals to keep up with the latest industry trends, market dynamics, and emerging technology. Attending workshops, seminars, and conferences provides professionals with vital insights into altering customer preferences, creative marketing methods, and developing industry best practices.
2. **Adapting to Regulatory Changes:** Updates to real estate rules, regulations, and compliance requirements are frequent. Continuing education keeps professionals up to speed on legal frameworks, licensing requirements, fair

housing legislation, and other regulatory developments that may affect their activity. Staying aware and in compliance with rules is critical for ethical behavior and avoiding legal ramifications.

3. **Enhancing professional abilities:** Professional development options help real estate professionals improve their abilities in negotiating, communication, marketing, and client service. By investing in skill development, professionals may increase their ability to serve customers, close agreements, and achieve successful transaction results.

4. **Expanding Knowledge Base:** Continuing education helps real estate professionals gain experience in specific areas, including commercial real estate, luxury properties, property management, investment analysis, and sustainable development. Professionals who acquire specialized expertise can differentiate themselves in the market and better respond to unique customer demands.

5. Professional development events and courses promote networking and cooperation among industry professionals, experts, and thought leaders. Networking allows people to

share their information, exchange ideas, and collaborate on projects or transactions. Developing a strong professional network may result in recommendations, collaborations, and new business prospects.

6. Maintaining professional credentials: Many states and regulatory agencies require real estate professionals to take continuing education courses in order to keep their professional licenses and certifications valid. Continuing education ensures that professionals complete ongoing education requirements and maintain good standing with regulatory agencies, allowing them to lawfully practice their profession.

7. Adopting New Technology: Professional development programs frequently involve introducing real estate professionals to new technology and digital tools that expedite company operations, increase productivity, and improve client experiences. Professionals may remain competitive in the digital age by learning how to use technology such as customer relationship management (CRM) software, virtual reality (VR) tours, and online marketing channels.

9. Continuing education fosters a culture of continual learning and personal growth for real estate professionals. Professionals adopting an attitude of continual learning and self-improvement, professionals may adapt to industry changes, overcome obstacles, and grab new opportunities for professional and personal growth.

To summarize, continued education and professional development are critical for real estate professionals to survive in a competitive and changing sector. Professionals can position themselves for long-term success and excellence in the real estate industry by staying up-to-date on industry trends, adapting to regulatory changes, improving professional skills, expanding their knowledge base, networking, maintaining professional credentials, adopting new technologies, and encouraging lifelong learning.

Conclusion

Beginning and growing a real estate firm necessitates a multidimensional strategy that incorporates a wide variety of information, skills, and techniques. Every part of the journey, from knowing the principles of the industry to managing legal issues, creating business strategies, and developing solid connections, takes careful preparation, devotion, and ongoing learning.

Throughout this thorough guide, we've covered the numerous aspects of starting a real estate business, such as market research, legal concerns, financial planning, branding, marketing, property purchase, management, and growth plans. Each phase of the process is critical for building a strong foundation and attaining long-term success in the competitive real estate industry.

Real estate entrepreneurs who have a proactive and solution-oriented approach may overcome obstacles, grasp opportunities, and position themselves for long-term success. Networking, continual education, and professional development are critical for remaining current with industry trends, developing partnerships, and improving abilities to match the market's increasing expectations.

Finally, success in the real estate sector involves a mix of strategic planning, flexibility, ethical behavior, and an unwavering dedication to providing outstanding value to customers. By accepting these concepts and executing the techniques provided in this guide, prospective real estate entrepreneurs can set out on their path with confidence, working to develop a successful and sustainable business in the dynamic world of real estate.

Reflecting on your journey

Reflecting on your real estate career is a great exercise that helps you to acquire insights, recognize accomplishments, and discover opportunities for development and progress. Here are some questions that can help you reflect on your journey:

1. What prompted you to seek a profession in real estate? Consider the motives and goals that prompted you to enter the real estate profession. Consider the things that drew you to this industry, as well as how your initial expectations have changed over time.

2. What have been the highlights of your journey thus far? Consider the triumphs, milestones, and noteworthy experiences of your real estate career. Celebrate your achievements and recognize the hard work, commitment, and persistence that have led to your

success.

3. What hurdles have you faced along the way? Consider the hurdles, disappointments, and problems you've encountered over your real estate career. Consider how you handled these problems, what you learned from them, and how they influenced your growth and resilience.

4. How have you developed personally and professionally? Consider the personal and professional progress you've made since beginning your real estate adventure. Consider the skills you've learned, the information you've acquired, and the ways you've grown as a real estate professional.

5. What have been your primary takeaways and insights? Consider the significant lessons and insights you've received from your real estate experience. Consider how these lessons have influenced your approach to business, decision-making, and client relationships.

6. "What achievements are you most proud of in your real estate career?"
Consider your finest successes and contributions to your real estate profession. Consider the influence you've had on clients,

coworkers, and the community, as well as the ways in which your work has helped others.

7. What are your future aims and aspirations? Consider your goals and objectives for your real estate profession's future. Consider the goals you intend to achieve, the areas you want to prioritize for growth and development, and the legacy you want to leave in the industry.

8. How do you intend to continue growing and improving your real estate experience?

Consider your continuing learning, professional development, and growth initiatives in the real estate sector. Consider how you intend to respond to changing market conditions, adopt new technology, and continue to develop your skills and knowledge.

9. What role do you envision yourself having in the larger real estate community?

Consider the influence you hope to make on the greater real estate community. Consider how you may help grow the industry through mentorship, activism, and the creation of a healthy and inclusive real estate environment.

10. What advice would you provide to someone beginning out in the real estate industry?

Consider the advice and insights you would provide to someone who is just starting out in the real estate industry. Consider the lessons you've learned, the values you believe in, and the advice you'd give to help them succeed and thrive in the field.

By reflecting on your real estate career, you may obtain useful insights, celebrate your accomplishments, and create a route for future development and success. Whether you are new to the sector or have been working for years, reflection is an important tool for personal and professional development. 10 Tips for Long-Term Success in Real Estate: Long-term success in the real estate sector demands a combination of strategic planning, perseverance, and ongoing learning.

Here are a few recommendations to help you continue and expand your real estate business in the long run:

1. **Forge strong connections:** Develop long-term connections with clients, coworkers, industry professionals, and community members. Focus on providing great customer service, maintaining open communication, and exceeding expectations. Creating a strong network of relationships may result in recommendations, repeat business, and beneficial

collaborations.

2. **Stay current with market trends:** Constantly monitor market trends, economic data, and regulatory developments affecting the real estate business. Keep up with developing technology, customer tastes, and demographic developments in your target market. Adapting to market dynamics and staying ahead of trends will allow you to make more informed decisions and stay competitive.

3. **Invest in education and training:** Decide to pursue lifelong learning and professional growth. Take advantage of educational opportunities, training programs, and industry certifications to improve your skills and knowledge. Stay updated on industry best practices, legal regulations, and technological advancements to stay ahead of the competition.

4. **Prioritize Client Satisfaction:** Strive to establish trust and credibility with your clientele. Listen to their problems, offer tailored solutions, and provide excellent service throughout the transaction. Customers who are satisfied with your services are more likely to recommend you to others and return later.

5. **Diversify Your Portfolio:** Consider diversifying your real estate portfolio by investing in a variety of assets, locales, and investment approaches. In changing market situations, diversification reduces risks while providing opportunities for development and stability. Consider residential, commercial, industrial, and multifamily buildings, as well as alternative investment vehicles including real estate investment trusts (REITs) and syndications.

6. **Manage Finances Wisely:** Prudent financial management and planning are essential for the long-term survival of your real estate firm. Maintain appropriate reserves for unforeseen needs, have steady cash flow, and avoid excessive leverage. Seek competent financial counsel as needed, and conduct frequent reviews of your financial performance to find opportunities for improvement.

7. **Adapt to Changing Technologies:** Use digital tools and platforms to simplify business processes, increase efficiency, and improve customer experiences by adopting technology. Use customer relationship management (CRM) software, property management systems, virtual tours, and online marketing methods to stay competitive in the digital era.

8. **Stay Ethical and Professional:** Always conduct oneself with integrity, honesty, and professionalism. Maintain ethical standards and legal regulations while putting your clients' best interests first. Building a reputation for ethical behavior and professionalism can help you gain trust and respect in business and with clients.

9. **Network and collaborate:** Attend networking events, industry associations, and community groups to broaden your professional network and form important partnerships. Collaborate with other real estate professionals, service providers, and industry experts to exchange ideas, resources, and possibilities for cooperation.

10. **Remain Resilient and Persistent:** Real estate is a dynamic and competitive profession that needs resilience and perseverance to overcome obstacles and achieve long-term success. Stay focused on your objectives, adjust to changing market conditions, and learn from setbacks and mistakes. Persistence and commitment are essential for overcoming hurdles and accomplishing your goals in real estate.